I AM DEXTER

I AM DEXTER

By Steve & Dr. Dru Pollinger, VMD

With Helayne Rosenblum

Copyright

Printed in the United States of America by IngramSpark

10 9 8 7 6 5 4 3 2 1 24 23 22 21

First Printing, **November 2021**

ISBN
Print 979-8-9850177-1-7
eBook 979-8-9850177-2-4

JEBWizard Publishing
37 Park Forest Rd.
Cranston, RI 02920
www.jebwizardpublishing.com

JEBWizard Publishing
Books with Character

Acknowledgments

"Until one has loved an animal, a part of one's soul remains unawakened."—
Anatole France

We would like to acknowledge the many dogs and cats that we have loved and cared for over 40 years together. We would not be the people that we are today without their presence in our lives.

As our young children were growing up, they competed with our furry companions for attention! We are thankful for their unabashed tolerance and how they have matured into hard-working adults with many animals of their own in their grown-up lives.

Our publisher has been accessible and patient, and we are grateful for his oversight.

Clients at the animal hospital have been so supportive - many know Dexter personally.

Tommy - we love you always. The lessons we learned after you left us so suddenly helped to bring *I Am Dexter* to life. Although you are gone, you are forever present.

Lastly, to Lolly - Steve's Aunt and Helayne's mother.

You are looking down on...us with a big smile!

Dedication

We are dedicating this book to Cathy Cloutier for her great work at the Upstate SPCA in Queensbury, New York and for uniting us with DEXTER - great and only choice!

She represents the best of all the people involved in rehoming animals nationwide.

Steve and Dru Pollinger

TABLE OF CONTENTS

PROLOGUE

Fate sometimes has a way of bringing together those who need healing. The expression "who rescued who?" is especially poignant in this extraordinary journey from tragedy to triumph. It is written from three distinct perspectives woven into one unforgettable story, proving that animals and their "humans" have an extraordinary bond.

Dexter, an abandoned dog who suffered unimaginable cruelty and inevitable post-traumatic stress (PTS) that has him physically and emotionally shut down, is miraculously saved and rehabilitated by the dedication and perseverance of the husband-and-wife team of Steve and Dr. Dru Pollinger. The Pollingers endured their own personal tragedy with the death of their son, making their willingness to help Dexter all the more remarkable.

Breaking down the walls of indescribable horror and pain Dexter suffered and his ultimate transformation from frightened animal to deeply loved and thriving member of the Pollinger "pack" is truly a story of hope born from adversity.

For forty years, the Pollingers have owned and operated the Fair Haven Animal Hospital in Fair Haven, Vermont. Daily, this devoted couple has worked to save countless animals from pain, suffering, and illness. In addition, they have taught their owners how to better parent their beloved pets. Written from the heart by Steve and Dru, with the additional perspective of Dexter, as the story unfolds, you will learn that this is a circle of love and hope as it brought healing to the rescuers as well as the rescued.

-Steve & Dr. Dru Pollinger & Helayne Rosenblum

FAIR HAVEN, VT

EARLY SUMMER 2018

What Have I Gotten Us Into?

Steve Pollinger

It's 4:30 p.m. on a Friday afternoon in mid-June. The phone is ringing, and our receptionist Lindsey has left for the weekend. Now it's my responsibility to answer the calls. Without looking at the caller I.D., my response is always unpretentious and unrehearsed.

"Fair Haven Animal Hospital, this is Steve – may I help you?"

"This is Cathy at the Upstate SPCA, and we have a potential adoption. The Irons have listed Dr. Pollinger as a reference; we need to verify that their current dog, Jeremy is up to date on his vaccinations and that they come in yearly for a wellness exam."

I promptly look at Jeremy's records and see that the shots are a bit overdue. Still, I remember these folks as wonderful people who would give a second dog a terrific home, and I tell her that. Cathy ignores my accolades about the family and robotically goes back to the timeliness issue of the vaccines.

It's the second call this week from a rescue group requesting vaccination histories.

Someone who knows me, not even well, would realize that this seemingly simple request will be responded to with impatience and annoyance.

I say to her bluntly, "Cathy, you've asked what should be the last question first. The problem is that every adoption agency asks the vaccination question first and always with the same boring tonality. The appropriate way, in my opinion, to find out about a prospective home for a pet is to initially ask about the humans as potential pet parents. Do they have the means to care for and the ability to fulfill a dog's needs? Do they walk their dog daily? Do they understand the terms exercise, discipline, and affection last? What kind of relationship do they have with my wife, Dr. Pollinger, and this animal hospital?"

Cathy absorbs my words…and seems to warm up to me as the conversation continues, so much so that my edginess dissipates. I feel as though we are developing a rapport. We talk for another twenty minutes or so about the dog overpopulation crisis, and ultimately, the Irons family will get their dog. I'm pleased with our newfound friendship and offer my services to foster a dog that can't be placed elsewhere because it has a history of extreme abuse.

I'm suggesting this particular scenario because I have a pack of my own calm, submissive dogs that will allow for and encourage the appropriate rehabilitation of a beaten-down dog.

This is not our first rodeo in working with troubled dogs and rehoming them. The world-renowned behaviorist Caesar Millan, aka *The Dog Whisperer*, paid me the biggest compliments at one of his seminars, praising my ability to build trust, loyalty, and love with my locally renowned Pitbull, Brooklyn. He also preached about the power of the pack. I know Cathy will remember this conversation, and I am on my way out the door.

2

I Am Dexter

My wife, veterinarian Dr. Dru Pollinger, and I have owned and operated the Fair Haven Animal Hospital in rural Vermont for 40 years. We have a wonderful relationship with our clients, giving us a unique perspective on people's lives and pets over generations! My role has been to deal with behavior issues and oversee the administration of the hospital. Together we are involved with a plethora of situations daily. Should the proposal I made to Cathy come about, we are equipped with the financial wherewithal, space, and dedication to carry it out.

NEW YORK, NEW YORK

AUTUMN 1964

A Burgeoning Steve

Steve Pollinger

Where in the world does this bodacious attitude of mine come from? Later that evening, while reflecting on the conversation I had with Cathy, a memory surfaced of one of my earliest experiences with a lost dog.

At age seventeen, while still living at home in Brooklyn (where I was born and raised), I was driving on the East River Drive in New York City one afternoon, and a loose dog zigzagged across the thoroughfare. Most New York drivers are not interested in traffic delays, period! The northbound three-lane highway had no shoulder on either side – just high cement barriers. How in the world a dog found itself in that position was baffling to me. Instinctively, I slowed down and began to block all three lanes with my Mercury Cougar.

I jumped out of the car. Horns were blasting, and I heard what I assumed to be a police siren in the background. The shepherd-mix dog was panicked and aimlessly ran back and forth. I knew I could capture him.

The fellow in the left lane… the lane of speed… was sitting in a brand-new black Cadillac. He exited the vehicle and was acting tyrannically.

"Move your fucking car – I'm late!" he screamed at me. "I'm not going to hit the dog!"

5

I realized that other cars would follow if I allowed him to go, and this dog would be roadkill. However, the siren was getting closer and coming in the opposite direction. I knew the police could give me the assistance needed to save this dog. Everything was playing out too fast.

The sharply dressed guy in the "Caddie," who was maybe forty-five years old, pushed me, then cocked his arm back to throw a punch. Big mistake! He didn't know that I had just won the New York City Golden Gloves in the middle weight division. I threw two punches and dropped him in full view of the stopped cars.

The police had now arrived on the scene. They hopped the median divider and assessed the situation. To my surprise, drivers from other vehicles got out and explained the circumstances to them to support my predicament. The "Caddie" fellow was detained and one of the officers handed me a rabies pole to help secure the dog. With all vehicles at a standstill, the dog was now making his way north in the middle lane.

Sensing I needed help, someone from one of the stopped cars ran up to me and handed me a sandwich. Game changer! As I jogged along at a slow pace, I unwrapped the sandwich, and held it down toward my left knee. "Here, boy," I said repeatedly. The dog slowed his pace, followed his nose, and was at my side. I calmly reached for his collar; no pole was needed - and we walked together back to my vehicle. As I opened my back door, one of the officers said, "I'll take the dog – it is policy. By the way, young fellow, you must know how to pack a punch because the guy in the Cadillac is bleeding pretty badly. We understand from interviewing the other drivers that you were just defending yourself in a perilous situation."

The second officer explained that they had a similar-looking family dog and would have appreciated someone saving his life. Little did I realize how this incident would impact me for the next fifty years.

At this time of my life I was studying acting, playing great pool, and successfully boxing. But big, exciting changes were on the horizon. Imagine me, "Brooklyn Steve," meeting, falling in love with, and marrying a veterinarian some day!

LAWRENCEVILLE, NEW JERSEY

SPRING 1981

A Young Resolute Dru

Dr. Dru Pollinger

My mother marched into the living room in her nightgown and slippers and stood looking down at me sleeping on the blue tapestry rug underneath the old piano. My arms cradled my newly adopted shepherd-dobie puppy.

"You're keeping this dog?" she asked in an enquiring, accusatory tone. It was six o'clock in the morning, on a Saturday!

The night before, I had arrived at my mom's apartment where I was temporarily staying (since I had no financial means to live anywhere else), dangling Rudy from the crook of my elbow. He had a large soft bandage on his right front leg, covering a degloving wound which could not be stitched. Four days prior, he had been hit by a truck in downtown Philadelphia. My three-week rotation through the Trauma Emergency Service at the University of Pennsylvania, School of Veterinary Medicine had brought us together. His original owner could not afford his hospital care and had willingly signed him over to the Vet School for adoption.

"Yes, mom, he is mine!" I exclaimed.

She did not look pleased – as she was not an animal lover.

It was more like she tolerated all the critters I brought into her life. She wasn't mean or uncaring – just standoffish when it came to connecting with them.

It was my father who truly enjoyed the cats and dogs that graced our family over the years. My dad made a $20 bet with me when I was six years old. Sitting across from him at the dinner table, I announced with the utmost sincerity, given my age, that I wanted to be a veterinarian someday. He loved my passion but did not believe that it was possible, given the family's financial circumstances. Sadly, he never knew that I succeeded. He died in 1974 from lung cancer when I was twenty-one. In my mind, even now I can see that $20 bill sitting on the old mahogany table in the dining room.

Needless to say, I could not leave the puppy and the kitten that I had rescued weeks earlier, with my mom during the day. She was particularly fragile since my father's death, and a bit detached from life. Taking care of two pets was out of the question. So, each morning for the last few weeks of vet school, I loaded Bogie the cat (named for Humphrey Bogart) in a carrier and the puppy, Rudy directly into the front seat of my car. It was an ancient, olive green Karmann Ghia with the customary split in the middle of the dashboard! Together we drove to the train station in Trenton, New Jersey, and boarded the passenger car filled with commuters riding to Philadelphia. Inevitably, Bogie would start meowing midway through the ride, which led to stares from people folding down their newspapers to see where the noise was coming from! At 30th Street Station, I then walked for twenty minutes with the cat carrier in one hand and Rudy draped over my shoulder to the vet school, where they were boarded for the day while I pursued my dream.

At night, the trip was in reverse, and my mom would be sitting at her kitchen window waiting to see me pull into the parking lot. I could not foresee that weeks later I would meet a sweet, handsome man from Brooklyn who loved dogs as much as I do. *CATS?* ... well...? Upon graduating and in very short order, we fell in love, were married, and two years later purchased an animal hospital in rural Vermont.

Steve & Dr. Dru Pollinger

FAIR HAVEN, VERMONT

MID-SUMMER 2018

The Call That Changes Our Lives

-Steve Pollinger

It was late afternoon on Friday, August 3, 2018, and we were preparing to leave work for a relaxing weekend. Just when we thought our day was done, Lindsey forwards a phone call from a woman named Florence Converse, asking for Steve Pollinger. "Hi, this is Steve," I say, and Florence begins to tell me a story.

"Hi Steve, I received your name from Cathy at the Upstate SPCA. I am the animal control officer in the town of North River, New York in the heart of the Adirondack Mountains."

She goes on to explain that for the past six months there have been numerous sightings and calls to her about a medium-sized red dog lost in the woods. The calls have all been virtually the same; that this dog appears to be starving and is fearful of any human contact. People were putting out food to entice him, but he would not approach until they were out of sight.

"There is no possibility of catching this dog! He is terrified of everyone," she says.

She continues to tell me that she finally, implored a local coyote trapper and animal rehabilitator, named Mark Laske, to help her and he was successful in live trapping the dog. He had attempted to domesticate him for a brief time at his home, but it was not working out.

"I've called a number of local humane societies and rescue groups. None are willing to take the dog in. Without any desire for human contact, he's unadoptable, but there is something about this dog in this situation that is tugging at my heartstrings.

"I'm at my wits end and took a chance in calling Cathy at the Upstate SPCA, which is some distance from here," says Florence.

She went on to explain that as she saw it, there were limited alternatives. The first was, euthanasia, "but I can't go there," she said. "If we try to place him in an adoptive setting, it would be to no avail because no one will take a dog that is terrified of being touched." She also thought of having him driven to *Friends of Animals in Utah* where he could live out a life in safety. They would certainly try for some rehabilitation, but the likelihood of rehoming him would be minimal.

Finally she took a deep breath and said, "Cathy told me about you Steve, your wife and your animal hospital – which gave me pause. I'm hoping this scared, scrappy, brown dog – so neglected and beaten down, with time and great patience could be rehabilitated. Could he end up living in a home with his own family? Will you consider trying?"

She truly sounded desperate and I could hear in her voice how much she wanted to get help for this dog.

I began to recall my conversation with Cathy earlier this summer and realize immediately that I may be in for more than I bargained for; however, I have never backed down from a challenge.

14

"Florence," I said with determination, "I'll give it my best and can assure you that no one will work harder than I."

She sounds relieved and elated, and we set up a time to transfer the dog on Monday morning. Now, I have to tell my wife about what is coming. Mind you, we have an animal hospital to run, a pack of four dogs, two cats and a flock of ten sheep. Thank God, our five kids are grown and out of the house.

Challenge Accepted

-Dr. Dru Pollinger

Following his phone call with Florence, my husband, Steve shared the news that he had agreed to try to rehabilitate an abandoned, abused dog that had no other options for help. So of course I supported that decision and within days we would be taking on a challenge and welcoming a new member to the pack.

The next day was a Saturday, and that morning, Steve and I employ Lindsey's "significant other" Mike to create a temporary enclosed space within the animal hospital, where the new dog can view all the activity that we encounter on a daily basis. This, in and of itself, will become the first part of his rehabilitation, and his new temporary home. Our plan is to immerse him immediately in the environment of the sounds, scents, and activities of the clients and their pets that the hospital provides. Steve will begin a training regimen, starting with a disciplined leash walk.

On a typical workday as a veterinarian, while I examine an animal, Steve provides training tips that help enrich the client's overall experience. We believe that this new dog will benefit from these personal interactions taking place right in front of him.

On Monday, August 6, 2018, at 10:00 am, Steve is in the reception area waiting for Florence, Mark Laske, and Dexter. Dexter is the name given to the dog by Mark. There is a level of excitement building in

16

anticipation of "the arrival." We purposefully have kept the waiting room clear so the introduction can be calm and positive for Dexter. The only visual of Dexter that we have is a picture emailed to us by Mark of a sighting in the Adirondack woods when Dexter was obviously on his last legs and weighing approximately 17 pounds. It was an emaciated framework of a dog, captured in time, camouflaged by leaves and trees, eyes staring blankly ahead. I will never forget that powerful and painful image.

As I write this story, a year and a half later, with Dexter's head in Steve's lap and his eyes fixated on my face, his current weight is 58 pounds!! Believe it or not, we have put him on a diet!

The Big Day

-Steve Pollinger

Through the big picture window of our animal hospital, I see an unfamiliar car pulling up to the front entrance. My plan was to have the leash handed off to me and immediately go for a walk that would begin to build a bond. Little could I have imagined the large crate that is carried out of the back of the vehicle and into the reception area.

In person, Florence is nicely dressed, fortyish, very sweet, with a concerned expression on her face. She introduces herself and Mark. Mark seems amicable, with somewhat of a more commanding presence. Our greetings being said, I am now anxious to meet Dexter who is confined in this cage.

I'm suspicious of the fact that he is not leashed. He appears terrified. He is standing up, head down, tail between his legs, ears hung low, and he is unwilling to make eye contact with me. Will this plan for an immediate walk be the right one? I don't think so, but I will try to engage him. Further conversation is not something that I am desirous of right now.

I say to Mark, "No leash?" He responds by pulling one from his pocket, opens the cage door, and with great difficulty, slides it around Dexter's neck. There is no aggression coming from him, but much more fear in his body language than I anticipated.

I Am Dexter

I take the leash and gently pull Dexter out. It is time for them to go and for me to begin my work. Florence hands me the paperwork regarding Dexter, and I let her know we'll be in touch.

"Dex" is reddish-brown in color and resembles a beagle lab cross. He is medium-sized with stout legs, a long, thick tail, and droopy ears – but it is his face and his gaze that grip you. Numerous puncture scars cover the lips, muzzle, and the fossa between his eyes. His tear ducts have been damaged, and he subsequently suffers from tear overflow. His right ear has a large black hairless patch where it folds over. The front legs show linear scars arranged in a diagonal pattern. The right hind limb has a two-inch black patch of skin that never healed properly. He walks clumsily with a subtle left front lameness and his hind-end sways, perhaps from hip or back trauma. His right rear toes drag when one watches his gait from behind. There are no visible marks on his belly or back. He never rolled over in submission! In his quest for food, he may easily have encountered raccoons or a bobcat – who knows? Could he have been hit by a car – possibly? Was he caught in barbed wire fencing?

We can only surmise, but we do know that no one was there to help him. His body slowly healed on its own, leaving only traces of the trauma he endured. Perhaps his earliest days were even worse, with beatings; as we will come to know with certainty later on, he was never socialized, only maligned. It is the hand approaching his face that terrorizes him.

After they leave, I take my typical deep breath, open the front door, and attempt to begin a short walk. Uh-uh! This dog is having none of it! He immediately starts writhing at the end of the leash like an alligator in a death roll, slithers down three stairs into the parking lot and under my parked car, dragging me with him. I'm thinking a walk is not appropriate right now! I have to find a gentle way to get Dexter back into the hospital.

Dru is in surgery with Lindsey assisting, but my son Brett, who runs a dog day care center at the back of our complex, coincidentally walks toward me. He realizes the urgency of the situation and runs over to help. Without thinking of the consequences, he crawls under the car, fearlessly grabs Dexter, pulls him out, picks him up, and carries this flailing, petrified dog back to the waiting room. I thank him and am relieved for the moment.

"Hey Dru, can you come to the waiting room?" I shout into the air. As she walks in, I bend down next to this emotionally exhausted canine and say, *"This is Dexter."*

She stands there, having heard the commotion, studying the dog, and contemplating the enormity of the task ahead of us. I slowly enfold him in my arms and carry him back to his newly constructed kennel, which has a window on one side and faces all the exam rooms on the other. I realize that he has never experienced "good touch."

His eyes were lifeless globes – large black circles embedded in a brown scarred face, staring straight ahead. He had no interest in engaging with his surroundings. He did not look at the two of us, but rather retreated into the corner farthest away from our presence. It is

20

said that the eyes are the windows of the brain. He is shut down, unwilling to be touched, wary of sound, asking to be invisible.

We stand there, hoping for a flash of interest, a spark that could be ignited – knowing immediately that there is no way to communicate. This journey will take a long time.

We leave him to soak in his new environment and adjust to it for the rest of the afternoon. At about 5:00 o'clock, before we leave for the day, Dru prepares his dinner. With deliberate slowness, she mixes the kibble and canned stew with her hands, so that he will associate food with her scent. At the same time, this process establishes her authority. She does this in front of Dexter to attempt to arouse his interest. The dish is placed in the front of the kennel area next to the water bowl. He lifts his head, but he does not approach the food until we back up a considerable distance. Dru turns on the radio to her favorite station – a mix of music and conversation – to comfort him for the evening.

Mulling Over Our Options

-Steve Pollinger

Our pack of four dogs wait in the office area/computer room in an adjacent building. We open the car door, they pile in, and home we go. Our evening begins with feeding the sheep, exercising and feeding the dogs, turning on the news, and preparing our own dinner.

We sit down to eat, and the conversation immediately turns to Dexter. Forget about any romance for us tonight!

As we talked, a light bulb goes on in my head! "Let's use Brooklyn (our 8-year-old Pitbull) to help in his rehabilitation, as soon as possible!"

Brooklyn was given to us at 7 weeks of age by a breeder in the area named Dennis. He was having difficulty selling his litter. Our family had suffered a tragic loss and this young man had wanted to make my wife Dru smile again by gifting her this sweet black and white puppy.

At the same time, there was a caveat to this gesture. If I were to train her to become a service dog, she would be a positive representative for this misunderstood breed. This would help Dennis sell additional pups in the future. Our plan to help Dexter was taking form! We had high hopes but we knew this would not be an easy road.

FAIR HAVEN, VERMONT

LATE SUMMER 2018

Brooklyn to the Rescue

-Dr. Dru Pollinger

As soon as Brooklyn came to live with us, Steve started working with her as a puppy. With great determination and commitment, she became a wonderful service dog. She is beloved by everyone, including Cesar Millan, for her trust and loyalty, gentle nature, and positive energy. She has a beneficial impact on any canine at the animal hospital, showing what true nonaggressive nature is.

Brooklyn is unaware of her power, and her gentility allows people to feel comfortable with this breed. Her job in the hospital, at times, is to help nervous dogs relax in the waiting room as well as the exam room. She has free rein to roam but doesn't overstep her boundaries. If another dog has aggressive tendencies, she will avoid any interaction. She is often our clue as to how to proceed.

Our dilemma this first night is formulating a plan for tomorrow, on how to get Dexter in and out of the confines of the animal hospital, through the back door, into the large fenced in exercise yard. One side of this grassy area has a long-shared fence with our son Brett's Woof Pack dog day care facility. We are hoping that Brooklyn can show Dexter the way. Tonight, however, Dexter is on the other side of town, contemplating his future.

I am Somewhere New…and I am Still Afraid

-Dexter

Why am I in this jail?

The air has other animal smells. I know it is a prison for dogs.

What is this music?

I hear hissing in the next room. Is it a bobcat like the one I had to fight in the mountains?

Who are these people? Why are they so interested in me?

There are no woods here to hide in. The hunt for food was always exhausting.

I am unsure.

This is too unfamiliar.

Who am I?

I am afraid of people.

I am afraid.

25

The blanket is soft. I will lay down in the darkness.

I am exhausted.

ADIRONDACK MOUNTAINS, NY

A FLASHBACK

MAY 2018

If Not for Mark Laske!

-Steve Pollinger

I would be remiss if Dru and I didn't share the back story as to how Dexter weathered hardship long enough to be able to survive and enter our lives. It all began with Mark Laske, a wildlife rehabilitator and coyote trapper. He is the person who finally captured Dexter in a *Have A Heart Trap* behind the Garnet Hill Lodge, an upscale Adirondack Hotel and Resort in North River, New York.

The hotel is surrounded by hundreds of miles of forest trails used for mountain biking, hiking, and nature enthusiasts. For a week or more, the chef from the lodge, Sebastian Martinez, who hailed from Puerto Rico, had noticed a skinny little red dog that kept coming around. A number of people tried to catch him, including the dog catcher, the grounds keeper, and various employees, but no one could! One of the staff knew of the plan to call Mark in case of a sighting.

On May 30, 2018, this well-known trapper was contacted, and he set his plan into action. A wonderful meal of mashed potatoes, gravy, and blueberries, personally prepared by Sebastian, was placed inside the trap. Within an hour, Dexter was "behind bars." Now the concern was the possibility of rabies being transmitted to anyone handling him. So, gloves were worn, and the cage was lifted into the vehicle for transport to Mark's home for an overnight stay in his garage. Physical contact was avoided. A mat was slid through the cage opening for his comfort, along with food and water.

The next morning, Dexter, who smelled like detritus after months in the woods, was driven to the Schroon River Animal Hospital for shots and a bath.

The vet tech, wearing gloves, pulled him out of the trap with a slip leash and did her best to clean up this terrified, struggling canine. She would later say she received a bath as well! He was physically restrained, tested for heartworm/ehrlichia/lyme and anaplasma (all negative, surprisingly) and vaccinated. A flea/tick spot on was dispensed along with worming pills to be placed in his food. Weighing in at a mere seventeen pounds and severely malnourished, a plan was made to repeat the vaccines in 3 weeks and neuter him if his weight improved significantly. Mark paid for this himself, hoping to foster the dog or keep him if possible. After feeding many small meals of ground venison or turkey mixed with dry kibble during the days that followed at his home, Dexter started to gain weight. He had a crate in a small room where the food was placed and access to an outdoor yard area where he could come and go. Physical contact was unthinkable.

Three weeks later, he was loaded once again into a car and driven to the vet's office for repeat vaccines, castration, and an overnight stay. Needless to say, absorbable sutures were placed. He now weighed thirty-four pounds!

FAIR HAVEN, VT

BACK TO THE PRESENT

LATE SUMMER 2018

Surviving but Puzzled

-Dexter

Back at the Fair Haven Animal Hospital, where I am now living, the sun is coming into the room. There are dogs barking on the other side of the wall.

When I was on the run and evading capture, the only peace came from an occasional nap in a sunny field. The sun brings me warmth and comfort. There are sounds and voices coming toward me now from the big space outside my cage. An older man and woman are calling "Dexter." It's the people from last night. The woman is mixing food again in front of me. My nose picks up that wonderful smell, but I remain still.

The man says, "Dru – are you ready?"

She replies, "Steve, you can open the cage door and let's see if he'll follow the food."

First Day of a New Life

-Dr. Dru Pollinger

As Dexter picks up his head, we slowly walk through the hospital corridor to the backyard, all the while calling his name. He watches motionless until we are fifteen feet ahead of him. Finally, his nose overrules his fear, and he cautiously begins to walk behind us, keeping a safe distance.

The door to the outside area is opened and the food bowl is placed on the grass. Steve and I walk away and wait, holding our breath. We are attempting to give him some SPACE because we recognize now that this dog is filled with fear and anxiety. We don't want to forcibly restrain him while he is so unaccepting of touch.

Time and patience will allow us to find a way to communicate with him. This endeavor is like taking a teenager from a rural farm in Kentucky and relocating him overnight into a hotel room in Hong Kong.

This is not at all like having a socialized puppy coming to live with you! We are only beginning to understand Dexter, but he has no way of understanding us – YET.

32

To our delight, he cautiously walks through the doorway into the yard and begins to sniff the perimeter. He ignores the food initially and we assume he's looking for an escape.

We are feeling pretty stupid when we realize he had to poop. He is not shy about doing this in front of us! Now he turns around, still keeping his distance, and jogs over to the food which he devours instantly. We've made the correct assumption that the sight, sound, and smell of Brett's Woof Pack Dog Daycare pack, on the other side of the cyclone fence, is lowering his anxiety level.

Thus begins day one. Steve gets two folding chairs from the hospital and we sit together, observing him as he explores the yard. We call his name intermittently, knowing that he will not come, but hoping it will bring recognition to that word. The back door remains open and we walk back inside to begin preparing for the day's appointments. It's a no brainer that Dexter will not follow!

Lindsey walks in promptly at 9:00 am and Steve discusses the protocol for the day. This is all done with Dexter's safety in mind. The doors to the exam rooms, typically left open, are now to remain closed. Lindsey will escort every client into a room, making sure there is no possible exit route to the front door for Dexter. The back door to the yard remains open, as it will have no influence on the activities in the hospital. Dexter stays outside by choice for the majority of the day. Our lives now become much more complicated.

We notice him from time to time peeking in at the exams-rooms, but he always maintains a distance, not wanting to interact with clients or other animals. Day's end is approaching – it's about 5 o'clock and we talk about making his dinner, which I proceed to do. Knowing this is our only way of communicating with him for now, I make a big deal preparing his food.

I create lots of noise opening the canned food, filling the water bowl, and mixing the dry kibble in with my hands – all the while talking softly, as Steve watches me, smiling.

Finally, Dexter appears in the doorway, enticed once again by his sense of smell. He is fed on the floor in his makeshift kennel without closing his door. I fill a Kong with peanut butter and leave it in the middle of the floor for his evening's entertainment. He lies down on his blanket. As we are leaving, we close the doors to the front office as well as the outside kennel area and depart for the evening. The radio is on, he has 1,200 square feet of space to explore in the dark, and some additional toys are laid out for him. We know that for a few more hours, he will hear the cars pulling up outside, as dog daycare clients pick up their dogs. The front windows face the entire parking lot, enabling him to watch, if he desires. As usual, we load our pack into the car from our office next door and home we go. As we drive the eight miles to our house in the woods, we both acknowledge at the same time how nice it will be someday to have Dexter with us. We do not know how long this rehabilitation process will take, but we are committed to the long haul. I laugh now as I think about how naïve we were then and Steve's impatience along the way.

Good Boy?

-Dr. Dru Pollinger

"Good boy" is an expression Steve abhors unless a dog has earned it. He dislikes it for the following reason. When a dog is exhibiting unwanted or aggressive behavior and clients try to squelch that conduct – they'll use the term "good boy," stroke the dog and in doing so create an even more unstable demeanor!

As Steve sees it, the term should be used ever so sparingly, and yet as we open the door to the animal hospital on day three, he surprisingly says "Good morning, Dexter, good boy!"

For the next few days we follow the same protocol – but on Saturday morning we introduce donuts and coffee! We sit relaxed in the backyard with no scheduled appointments to interrupt us, coffee cups in hand. Steve, as usual, is getting impatient with our slow progress, while Dexter continues to keep his distance. He breaks off a piece of his donut, extends his arm, and calls to Dex.

"Here, boy!"

Dexter saunters closer to our chairs, venturing inside the mental perimeter that he has maintained for a week. He is definitely interested in the new food! To our understanding, he has not taken food directly from a human hand. He gently grabs his share of the donut and backtracks to his safe distance. Somewhere behind that blank stare is a willingness to make an ever so slight connection with us.

35

Now, my husband of forty years goes into one of his tirades. "Dru, I realize that this dog's previous owner has enticed him with food only to beat him!!"

He continues to go on relentlessly about the torture that Dex has most certainly endured, wishing that that "*mother----er*" would someday come out to claim him. Steve's fighting days have never left him. Even at this early stage we have a little glimpse of Dexter's past; physical abuse he could no longer endure. Breaking a chain, running, and becoming disoriented in that dense forest was a probable provenance, as we see it.

Several weeks passed and Dexter's inability to adapt to genuine human kindness was disconcerting. Although he counted on us for food, he would not allow us to pet him anywhere, nor would he come to us willingly unless a treat was involved. Steve's desire to first build trust and loyalty dissuaded him from using his typical methods of training a dog to come. A fifteen-foot-long lead was out of the question at this time, because Dexter was terrified of being approached by a human. A whistle or clicker elicited no response.

Shut down dogs… those with a history of psychological trauma and physical abuse, often require the help of another dog to facilitate rehabilitation. So, Steve and I continued to follow our morning routine with Dexter in the exercise yard, but now introduced Brooklyn, the Pitbull, to the mix. Her energy was perfect, but we knew it would be. She allowed Dexter to sniff her in typical meet and greet fashion, and his interaction was appropriate. He seemed to have no conflict with other canines. He followed her around and observed her playful

36

behavior along the fence line, with the pack of daycare dogs on the other side. In observing her demeanor with us, he began to come closer to our chairs as long as Brooklyn was in between. In his mind, she became his guardian!

While Steve distracted him with a piece of donut, I was now able to scratch his butt! Thus, began what we would later call "the Dexter dance routine," a real breakthrough moment. As silly as it seems and looks, he would wiggle his hind-end from side to side, treading his back feet, while lifting his head into the air and swinging it back and forth. For the first time, he seemed to enjoy the human touch. Brooklyn now begged for her piece of donut! Of course, realize that this slight acceptance of our hand was just that – SLIGHT!

As the authors of this book, it by no means gives us permission to call ourselves "experts" in the term others might use to describe Dexter's condition. Forty years of hands-on experience with dogs, our extensive reading, and discussions with academics, should qualify us to equate this dog's behavior, to PTSD, a human condition. But we cannot do that, nor should anyone. There isn't a way to translate an <u>unknown</u> past evil event in this dog's life, into words. He can't tell us. Going even further, those words are not easily come by in humans. That being said, Cesar Millan's famous quote that *"Dogs live for the now"* seems correct; because despite significant behavioral signs of past trauma, Dexter looks only for the basics of survival – food, more food, and shelter. Packs of animals, roaming the streets of for instance, Mexico City, don't have psychiatrists to discuss their problems with. They find their place in a pack, be it the middle or back, and look to move forward. Front of the pack dogs don't have these psychological issues, as they are the leaders and instinctively guide the group.

The Psychiatry Behind Psychological Trauma

-Dr. Dru Pollinger

Dexter entered our lives in a state of helpless disconnection – a mangled canine soul unable to interact on a social level. We were unable to communicate with him, unable to touch him, unable to soothe him with our compassion. His startle response was off the scale and he isolated himself in the nearest corner he could find, avoiding contact with people. He simply sat and stared blankly ahead or laid down disinterested in his environment. Food was his salvation. Sleep was his escape.

There is a growing body of scientific evidence that animals can experience PTS. The condition cannot be equated with post-traumatic stress disorder (PTSD) in humans for the following reason. Human PTSD is a well-defined diagnosis based on criteria contained in the *Diagnostic and Statistical Manual of Mental Disorders* (DSM-5). According to this psychiatric bible, PTSD begins with a stressor or traumatic event. Four distinct symptom clusters are outlined, and these symptoms must persist for at least a month. They are as follows:

Re-experiencing (previously called "intrusive recollection.") – involves the persistent re-experiencing of the experience through thought or perceptions, images, dreams, illusions or hallucinations, dissociative flashback episodes or intense psychological distress or reactivity to cues that symbolize some aspect of the event.

39

Avoidance (previously called "avoidant/numbing") – involves avoidance of stimuli that are associated with the trauma and numbing of general responsiveness. This is determined by avoidance of thoughts, feelings, or conversations associated with the event and for avoidance of people, places, or activities that may trigger recollections of the event.

Negative Cognitions and Mood (new in the DSM-5) – involves negative alterations in thought and mood as characterized by symptoms like inability to remember an important aspect of the event(s), persistent negative emotional state, persistent inability to experience positive emotions and others.

Arousal – (previously called "hyper-arousal") – involves alteration in arousal and reactivity. Examples of this include irritable behavior and angry outbursts, reckless or self-destructive behavior, hypervigilance, exaggerated startle response, concentration problems, and/or sleep disturbance. (DSM-5, 2013)

No one can evaluate manifestations in animals that correlate with many of the above symptom clusters. Dex could not talk to us about flashbacks, hallucinations, or dreams. He could not possibly describe conversations or intrusive thoughts. He could not tell us about his feelings. We could recognize his fear of people and touch by his avoidance behavior. We could recognize his hypervigilance and his extreme startle response. He had generalized fear.

In a paper entitled "Psychological Trauma in Animals" included in the World Small Animal Veterinary Association Congress Proceedings, 2018, Franklin D. McMillan, DVM, DACAW writes:

40

"Current research has identified the primary physiological system involved in PTS to be the hypothalamic-pituitary-adrenal (HPA) axis, which appears to undergo pronounced and persistent dysregulation. Studies of PTSD show that fear is the key emotion involved in the disorder and the adaptive functioning of fear conditioning, with the capability to distinguish between safe and unsafe stimuli and facilitate identification of danger, fails in this disorder. Rather than a normal level of alertness with relaxed attention, individuals with PTSD have an elevated baseline of arousal: the individual suffering from PTSD continues to function in a "red alert" status of readiness, behaviorally primed for another stressful event. To severely affected individuals, almost every place becomes perceived as unsafe, resulting in a loss of one's sense of security."

Does Dexter Have PTS?

-Dr. Dru Pollinger

While not being able to call Dexter's behavior PTSD definitively, we can certainly name his disorder as PTS. His fear persona is related to his past suffering. By watching his demeanor in a new, safe, loving environment and observing his response to new stimuli, we can gather clues about his previous life.

Dogs can be severely stressed in any number of ways, all of which have the potential to create PTS. Imagine the scenarios that can be considered sources for psychological trauma: dogs used in the fighting ring, dogs involved in vehicular accidents, dogs kept in confinement for extended periods of time, certainly dogs that are physically and verbally abused, dogs that are attacked by other animals, dogs lost in natural disasters, military dogs returning from combat experience, dogs used for testing and research, working dogs that are pushed too far, dogs that are rehomed multiple times, dogs that are kept in hoarding environments, dogs that are neglected and abandoned, dogs that become lost in an unfamiliar area, and the list goes on.

Steve and I now have a medical name for what Dexter is exhibiting but the path forward, in terms of therapy, is on us.

Dr. Bruce Perry and Maia Szalavitz authored a book in 2006, called *"The Boy Who Was Raised as a Dog."* Dr. Perry is an American psychiatrist and founder of the Child Trauma Academy and adjunct

42

Professor in the Department of Psychiatry and Behavioral Sciences at the Feinberg School of Medicine at Northwestern University. He is known for his creativity and sensitivity in working with severely traumatized children, some of whom are non-verbal. The book consists of eleven true stories which describe his interactions and experiences with children suffering from sexual and physical abuse to survivors of Waco, to a boy raised as a dog.

He says, "One of the defining elements of traumatic experience…particularly one that is so traumatic that one dissociates because there is no escape from it – is a complete loss of control and a sense of utter powerlessness. As a result, gaining control is an important aspect of coping with traumatic stress. To develop a self, one must exercise choice and learn from consequences. The process needs to be self-directed and the child (client) needs to be in control of the timing." Further on, he remarks, "What is needed is presence, appropriate timing (pace), structure not rigidity and nurturance but not forced affection." He is compassionate, patient, kind and respectful in his writing and above all, inspiring. He was beautifully articulating the way that Steve and I, intuitively were attempting to bring Dexter back to life. Yes, Dexter is a dog, not a person, but these principles should be universal. Let the dog have some control, let the dog make choices, let the dog control the pace. We, as rehabilitators, should have rules and gentle consequences, and above all, be very patient and creative.

To Pee or Not To Pee?

-Dr. Dru Pollinger

The outside exercise yard is wonderful for Dex, but as the weather grows colder, he is spending more time inside the animal hospital by choice, and I recognize that he has a potential medical problem. He has an insatiable desire for water and is peeing everywhere.

Lindsey and I are constantly cleaning up after him in between exams and surgery! The hospital floors have never been so clean. I am not telling Steve any of this to save myself some grief. He absolutely adores me and trusts my judgment medically speaking, but he will not be able to grasp the significance of this issue.

It would be almost impossible for Dexter to live inside a home if he is not housetrained, and so I must determine the cause and ultimately work with my husband to solve the problem.

At first, my thinking was that it could be related to the fact that he had never been in a house and/or that he was simply marking his new territory, but his water drinking was excessive! I'm still not sure if this is behavioral or medical and begin running simple tests to find an answer. Numerous urinalyzes during the day confirm that he IS able to concentrate his urine, which is a good thing, and that he probably does not have diabetes mellitus or a urinary tract infection. Now, however, I have to run extensive lab work to rule out all the

44

possibilities. This means we will have to restrain him to take blood, and I am worried this will set him back mentally.

Steve, with a donut in hand, is able to grab Dex's collar after cornering him, and lifts him onto the exam table. He freezes in Steve's arms, showing no signs of aggression; there is only fear in those dark eyes.

The blood is taken without a struggle and sent out to the laboratory. Ultimately, after ruling out numerous causes of PU/PD (polyuria and polydipsia), a diagnosis of central diabetes insipidus is confirmed. Now that I have an answer, I know how to treat him medically, I can save on my cleaning bill, and look forward to some normalcy when he is in a home environment.

I put Dexter on DDAVP (Desmopressin) oral tablets at a starting dose of .1mg three times daily. His urinary behavior improved immediately and although he still needed to urinate in the middle of the night, I knew it would be possible for me to cope with this in our home.

I am an insomniac and up at least three times nightly! I gradually decreased his meds to twice a day and then halved his morning dose to achieve medicating him with the lowest possible amount of drug and still having the desired effect! Success at last!

It is very possible that Dexter's medical problem arose from repeated head trauma. His numerous facial scars lend credence to this, and although we will never know, his fear of having his face approached by a hand advances this theory.

FAIR HAVEN, VERMONT

OCTOBER 2018

Step by Step…. The Pack Steps In

-Dr. Dru Pollinger

It's the beginning of October and Steve is getting a bit frustrated because Dexter needs to be leash-trained and walked. It's the first tenet in creating a calm, submissive dog.

Exercise, through a disciplined walk, drains negative energy and is the precursor of rules, boundaries, and limitations – a Cesar Millan principle. We are hoping to teach him to come by following this regimen.

Once again, using the donut now as bait and the butt scratch as a distraction, Steve is able to grab Dexter's collar and attach a leash. He is accepting of the leash hanging from his neck, and we allow him to drag it around the exercise yard on his own for several mornings. In short order, I begin picking up the handle end and allow Dexter to lead the walk with Brooklyn at his side. His "alligator" behavior is now a thing of the past, but the proper walk is yet to come. Mike Jones, Lindsey's boyfriend, is beginning some construction work and painting in this very same yard. He is extremely shy and quiet, which suits Dexter just fine, and so another human-canine bond is created! We've also incorporated two more of our dogs into Dexter's life, helping him to become a member of our family pack.

One, is an eleven-year-old rescued golden retriever, named Chomper, who also came from a traumatic environment nine years ago. He has a facial scar above his big black nose which resembles a set of human upper teeth.

Here is his story: To properly run a successful animal hospital, Steve and I must address community concerns. We had received numerous complaints about a dog named Chomper living in front of a man's house, near where we live in the country.

Forced to fend for himself day and night, constantly seen in the road dodging traffic, the neighbors were concerned he would be hit by a car. We were told that he was not allowed in the house, and there was no shelter from inclement weather, nor was there a fenced yard to keep him safe.

One of the neighbors, who happens to be the town judge, alerted Steve to the fact that this dog's owner was physically abusive to him. We were baffled that nothing had been done by this judge. A judge? The local police department had given Steve permission to do what he had to, in situations like this. This was a show of respect to the hospital, for its help in rescuing three pitbulls from a dog fighting ring. The officers were able to arrest the culprits but were reluctant to retrieve the dogs from their confinement in a basement. We were able to accomplish the task.

So, we took it upon ourselves to investigate this dog's living conditions. Steve stopped by the owner's house to discuss what he had heard and prefaced the conversation by explaining that we owned the animal hospital in town.

I Am Dexter

At first, it seemed to us that the owner, in the current situation, was simply uneducated about how to care for a dog, and Steve left him with a directive to keep him housed, well fed, and walked. Unfortunately, the complaints kept coming in, and the owner was revisited. This happened several more times, until one snowy December evening, when Steve was driving home and swerved off the road to avoid hitting Chomper.

He got out of the car, pounded on the man's door, and asked him to come outside. The guy was about six feet five inches tall and built like a truck! Trying to avoid an altercation, Steve suggested that the dog be rehomed with our pack. The guy reluctantly acquiesced but wanted $100 as a trade-off. The money was handed over, avoiding a fistfight, and Chomper became a Pollinger.

The second dog helping Dexter is named Harvey, and she was rescued from the hurricane in Texas, after which she is named. Our youngest daughter, Tess, was involved in the animal rescue effort there. The dog was grabbed by Tess while floating on a tire in a submerged gas station parking lot. Her recovery was rather immediate with good veterinary care (if I say so myself) and a loving home. This twelve-pound Chiweenie found it very easy to bond with Dexter and he to her. Just like many soldiers who come home from war and adjust to civilian life fairly easily, some experience severe PTSD for years, if not forever. So, as we recount Dexter's story, he is one dog that cannot easily relinquish his horrors. The backyard has now become a "safe haven" for Dex, with Mike and three of our four dogs present during the day.

Steve is forever looking to speed up the rehabilitation process of this fearful new member of our family. We are no longer planning to foster and rehome Dexter. Instead, he has found his "forever" place, just as Florence had hoped!

Changing Leaves and Changes to Come

-Dr. Dru Pollinger

Vermont in the fall is one of the most beautiful places in the world. The leaves are changing in mid-October – the amazing red, yellow, and brown colors come into view and the cool, brisk air draws many thousands of visitors to the state.

At the animal hospital, we meet tourists and their pets with an array of issues, including porcupine interactions, forgotten medicine scenarios, lost dog situations, and everything in between. I have always enjoyed spending time with new clients from out of the area and the conversations that ensue are fascinating.

Our *"Dexter from the Adirondacks"* story is now incorporated into the exam room experience and all want to meet him up close and personal! Steve is encouraging this interaction to further help Dexter's recovery.

His black nose peeking through the doorways, without allowing the appropriate touch that people are seeking, is like offering an ice cream cone to a child but not letting them eat it! More often than not, Dexter is curious for a moment, but then retreats to the outside yard, leaving everyone wanting more – with Steve promising the client a copy of the forthcoming book!

He is so happy with what we have accomplished thus far. I suppose, in his heart of hearts, he would have liked to "one up" Cesar

51

by having Dexter walking appropriately in a shorter period of time. However, a previous, very serious back surgery has undermined his physical ability to walk distances at a brisk pace.

He is a very proud man, and so initially, we both began walking Dexter around the yard in a somewhat disciplined fashion. Steve is already planning to take him on a mile long walk in a week! Despite the fact that we have finally been able to leash him, he continues to be tremendously fearful of touch and will not come to us on command. We are still tricking him to grab his collar and another new issue arises. We have some concerns about his excessive gagging when the leash is taut – a possible throat issue from some prior trauma?

We gently leash walk the yard on a daily basis for about a week. I recognize that we needed to have some fun with this process, so I began chanting a sentence from a TV commercial for Shriner's Hospitals for Children. The particular scene is of a young child with prosthetic legs delighting in his new ability to walk.

"I'm walking, I'm walking," he cries to his mom.

"You are walking!" says his mom.

This endearing image comes into my mind as Dexter, Steve, and I move around the yard. "We're walking, we're walking," I sing to him gently and he seems to respond to my "happy" energy. My husband is adamant about a dog having a positive response to healthy energy and body language.

As a new week begins, Steve's plan for the mile long walk goes into effect. It begins in the backyard, and together Steve and Dex go

through the gate leading to the front of the hospital and continue to
the sidewalk following the main road.

Let's Go For a Walk

-Steve Pollinger

When I train a dog to walk, the goal is to have him directly on my left side or one pace behind. Despite some physical limitations, which I generally ignore, I move forward with Dexter using gentle pulls upward on the leash and together we develop a kind of rhythm. There was consistency in this process; but sporadic. He would follow his nose sideways away from me, suggesting that old fear issue of restraint.

Sometimes he would twist his head from side to side to remind me that he still had an air of control! Alternatively, he would lean hard into my leg for several strides, alerting me of his desire for protection and comfort. The noise of the eighteen-wheelers passing did not faze him in the least, nor did bicycles or pedestrians approaching us. I continued this daily routine throughout the week while Dru was seeing patients or doing surgeries.

One afternoon as I began the walk, my son Brett approached, commenting on how well Dex was doing and asked to join me. Typically, I would be at curbside for about a half mile, then cross over to the opposite side of the road and return to the hospital parking lot – all the while allowing Dex to intermittently smell and pee. On this particular day, I stumbled on uneven ground, which evoked a startle response from Dexter. In the confusion of the moment, I fell as he pulled away in fear and a link on his collar broke, freeing him.

I Am Dexter

With an immediate reaction to seeing the dog loose in the road, Brett threw himself on Dex to protect him – thinking of Dexter first, which I respected. Together we got up, regrouped, converted the leash into a collar, smiled, and with a sigh of relief, made our way back to the parking lot. We were all okay, but the incident affected me subconsciously.

My son Brett incurred a chin laceration from his intentional flat fall on the dog to shield him. I don't believe that Dex would have run, but I wasn't confident enough to test that theory yet.

Over a fifty-year period, I have purchased and used every type of training collar imaginable. My disappointment with this one breaking fueled my subsequent call to the big chain store in the area (known for pet supplies) where I bought it.

Their response to my maligning their inferior product was perfunctory. IT IS BECAUSE I WAS FALLING IN LOVE WITH THIS DOG and realized the possibilities of his being hurt that I went into a tirade. I looked at Dru coming toward me as I was on the phone and knew better than to allow my temper to get the best of me.

She has a calming influence on me. For sure, I would have been an "out of control" guy if she had not come into my life. She now helped me to move forward, and I did.

From that point on, I went back to using my thirty-five-cent leash/collar in one, and to this day have never had another incident. How in the world I bought into the "new dog, new collar" tradition is beyond me.

The Comforts of Home

-Dr. Dru Pollinger

Dexter has adapted to the hospital routine remarkably well. He enjoys having the freedom to go in and out through the back door at will, but as the temperature drops into the thirties and forties during the day, we are forced to close the outside door to the exercise yard.

Dex is now spending more time in the kennel area at the back of the hospital. At the end of each day, when feeding him, I am attempting to help him overcome his fear of having his face touched. I start by encircling the food bowl on the floor with my feet while he eats, and after several days, switch to using my hands to hold the dish and lifting his meal to knee level, while sitting on a chair.

One evening, I gently move my thumbs upwards to his lips as he is eating; ever so slightly, they touch his soft muzzle and for the first time, he is allowing it. I can feel his body energy through my fingers. What an amazing breakthrough for me – to calmly stroke his skin while he is so absorbed with his dinner! My patience has been rewarded and I know in my heart that this dog will become my *BFF*.

In order to encourage Dexter to spend more time in the exam room area, we bring a sofa from our home to the animal hospital and place it where Dex's original makeshift kennel was constructed. Up to this point, he has been sleeping on blankets on the floor.

A Heartwarming Reunion

-Dr. Dru Pollinger

It's almost November 1st and we're hoping to have our "new dog" home and part of our pack by the end of the year.

This new sofa area becomes a beehive of activity during the day now. Steve is occasionally falling asleep on it, some of my clients have conversations with me while sitting there, and even some of their dogs are enjoying jumping on the cushions!

In comes Harvey for a visit, and she immediately hops up and takes over half of it. Next comes Brooklyn, and the two of them are fixtures sitting next to each other, whenever they are allowed in. Dexter is ever-observant, and we are wondering when HE will make himself comfortable. Thank goodness, his peeing behavior is better controlled with medication and his demeanor inside is more relaxed. Hopefully, he will sleep on the sofa at night when he is alone.

A few days pass, and one morning we see his dried muddy footprints on the cushions. It had rained the night before, just prior to letting him in, and the evidence of his enjoying the new "bed" was unmistakable! The comforts of home.

My husband's sofa naps are becoming more frequent with the cold weather. I realize this is really a ploy to have Dexter interact with him more in the hospital, in a calm, submissive state of mind. So, when

Dexter begins to lie down on the floor next to the sofa, Steve starts dangling his arm off the cushion, resting his hand gently on Dexter's neck. This is another major breakthrough and becomes routine over the next few days.

One afternoon while Steve is truly sleeping, as I come out of surgery, Dexter is on the sofa between Steve's legs, snoring! He has chosen this comfort behavior on his own and this now becomes the norm. We see that his fear of us is gradually diminishing and consider it a milestone, but only one of many that must come.

Feeling that Florence Converse (Dexter's savior) would enjoy hearing about his progress, Steve initiates a phone call, inviting her to come by at her convenience. Mind you, she lives almost 2 hours away, but she is very willing to visit. Surprisingly, the next afternoon on a windy, overcast fall day, when we both begin a walk with Dexter, we see her car turn into the parking lot.

She is thrilled to see him and able to greet him with a pat! Just recently, he has been allowing people to gently touch him when he is leashed. She joins us on the walk, but as we start out, the weather doesn't cooperate and it begins to pour, soaking the four of us! – We are all laughing now! As we enjoy this memorable moment in the rain, her smiling face tells it all – for it was she, with her determination, that saved this abandoned dog from euthanasia. How gratifying to have this first reunion.

He Thinks He Owns the Place!

-Dr. Dru Pollinger

The hospital reception area leads via a corridor to three exam rooms on the left of the passageway, while large windows overlooking the parking lot are on the right. All of these rooms are open and visible to the laboratory and pharmacy sections. This set up allows the staff to interact openly with the doctor and pets being checked out, while fulfilling their duties – including dispensing medications, running lab assays, and updating records.

The first exam room caters to small dogs, cats, and exotics. The second room is for larger dogs where they can step onto a platform, be weighed, then raised up electronically. The sound of this moving scale is unmistakable but not harsh. The third room is for overflow! The x-ray room, dog kennel area, tub room, cat compartments, surgery and isolation cages surround the perimeter. So, really, it is one giant circle for foot traffic, which by now Dexter can navigate as well as I can – but he is much faster.

What is fascinating is that he has totally ignored the front windows for months now. Only dogs that have never lived inside would exhibit this disinterest. One evening as we are leaving, I remarked to Steve that "hopefully, someday soon, he will be at the windows and barking, wanting to come home with us!"

Seemingly overnight, Dexter becomes assertive in the animal hospital. He owns everything and everything is his – including me! The tenet that Steve used regarding exercise and discipline has been ignored by us up to this point because the dog was so fearful, and we had to show him patience and love first.

Now there are always other ways of accomplishing a challenge, and Steve is not saying his is the only way, but as you'll see, it's beginning to work out in a positive fashion.

Maybe I Shouldn't Have Waited This Long

Here Comes Malchus

-Dr. Dru Pollinger

Had Malchus met Dexter when he was mentally weaker, the introduction may have gone much smoother! Malchus first presented at the animal hospital as a six-month-old pup, for vaccinations. He was a third dog for a young couple with too much on their plate!

He immediately took to Steve in the reception area, with his silly look and clownish behavior, yet when Steve wanted his attention and did his famous "touch" with his foot, Malchus was as focused a dog as Steve had ever seen. He absolutely adored a baby in the waiting room, and to this day he will go through an open car window to lick a child.

At a training session one afternoon, Steve leashed Malchus to a baby stroller, and he immediately walked perfectly in step with the mother and child. He instinctively was very protective of children. Due to this immediate bonding with Steve, this young couple wanted my husband to take him. At that particular time, we were both overwhelmed with family responsibilities and could not commit. Six months later, when we were in a better position to adopt him, he was living with another couple but in a deplorable situation. He was not kenneled—he was caged twenty-three hours a day—and had not yet been neutered.

The original owners, who were paying to have the surgery done, implored Steve to adopt him. DONE DEAL!

This fawn boxer with one ear missing (we never knew the true story) and the face of an angel immediately connected with Brooklyn and Chomper.

His name was biblical in origin. The story goes that Malchus was the slave of the High Priest, Simon Peter. Peter drew his sword and cut off his servant's right ear (John 18:10). It seemed appropriate to keep his name, although our Malchus was missing not his right, but his left ear! He learned to walk at Steve's side in two hours and although he fit in well with our pack of dogs, he was not thrilled with our big black cat – HMMM! However, over time, our furry feline and Malchus reached a truce.

Training is a Family Effort

-Steve Pollinger

A year and a half before Dexter's arrival, our oldest son, Brett, left a corporate job in Washington, D.C. and returned home. He could not deal with a desk and a phone, having always been an outdoors guy!

I pride myself on being a foreseer of trends and suggested to Brett to open a dog daycare center in a building that we owned adjacent to the animal hospital. Not only was the building large enough, but the surrounding acre of lawn was perfect for a first-class operation. He studied hard and spent time with my friend Cesar Millan, honing his skills further in January 2016 by attending Cesar's intensive training seminars in south Florida for a week.

In the spring of 2016, Brett opened Woof Pack, the most successful dog daycare operation in the state. My observation and evaluation of these facilities will be forthcoming in our next book!

That being said, I was beginning to find myself in a somewhat diminished physical capacity, given my age, so I rely on his accomplished abilities in training and work with him on difficult cases. Fortunately, my wife and I have the ability to keep our dogs (our pack) with us all day.

Brooklyn, as mentioned earlier, serves as an ambassador for nervous or fearful dogs that come into the hospital. A good deal of the time our pack will horse around and take long walks with me.

One memorable day a well-meaning staff member from the dog daycare center opened a shared gate between Woof Pack and the animal hospital. This gesture was meant to allow Malchus to play with some high energy dogs, but it went awry.

Immediately, Malchus was attacked by a Rottie (Rottweiler) named Delgatto. Within moments, Malchus was on top of the dog and dominated the situation. After this interaction it took me some time to help him understand that this was an isolated incident; from that point on, he has been somewhat guarded (not with our pack) but alert with new, powerful dogs. I can read his body language quicker than the blink of an eye.

So, with him, unlike Brooklyn, introductions are made face to butt, giving him clues to the dog's sex and energy, and in his mind, "Where have you been and what have you eaten?" If that momentary exchange is anything but positive, I will be a bit more dominant in handling him, insisting that he be more submissive and accepting. Knowing this about him had delayed my introduction of Dexter to him.

Now, as smart as I think I am, I ask my son to come into the exercise yard that Dexter has become accustomed to and that Malchus plays in from time to time. Together we will oversee the introduction. How could I have ignored or forgotten the fact that this yard borders the dog daycare center with a cyclone fence and high energy dogs on the other side? It's a horrible choice of location for this "meet and greet," and to make matters worse, I allow both dogs to come running out from different doors!

64

I Am Dexter

I stop here to reflect upon an incredible scene with actor Paul Newman in the movie "The Color of Money," where he accepts and plays in a big stakes pool game that is out of his league at that moment in time. He then exclaims to Tom Cruise, as his eyes tear up, "How could I have been so foolish?"

How can I have been so foolish? This introduction looked more like the opening bell of the first-round of a boxing match! Neither dog was leashed, and they began to fight. It was my fervent desire to have everyone get along that drove my impatience. Even this old man can live and learn.

The fact that I was careless in this initial meeting did not thwart my confidence to establish a relationship between these two dogs. Brett, on the other hand, had reservations, but this did not deter me one bit. I did know what to do and my instincts were correct.

Both dogs were to walk with me for a mile and a half twice a day. Malchus was to be leashed first, as he was a senior member of our pack. Dexter was to observe and be leashed second. Once leashed, there was no antagonism. Walking through the doorways had to be done with precision. Human first, senior dog second, new dog third and I MEAN in that order only. I was establishing a family or a pack hierarchy. As the walk commenced, I didn't vary from my position as "general" with the "troops" a step behind.

This type of disciplined walk allowed them to interact without any conflict whatsoever. They were focusing on the walk under my direction. This process became an absolute daily ritual, rain or shine. They became anticipatory of this healthy routine. Their respect for each other continued to grow, and I looked forward to using my positive energy and body language to further their bonding and prevent any future conflict when Dex finally comes home with us.

Our Pack Is Bonding With Dexter

-Dr. Dru Pollinger

Steve and I are in a happy place. Things are going well, so much so that Dexter now has supervised visitation with all four of our dogs in the office space where they normally spend time during the day. The power of the pack! I cannot express enough how meaningful the terms energy and body language are to a pack of dogs. Dexter has taken the proper steps forward despite the fact that he is still wary of affection. We believe that will come, but it is more important that the pack as a whole and individually, respect and follow Steve's direction. Malchus has certainly learned to accept our new addition.

Back in the animal hospital, Dex now wants to be included in my job examining animals! Where in the past he has stayed unobtrusively in the background, NOW he wants to be a part of the action.

The whirring sound of the weight scale moving up and down in the second exam room incites a new reaction from him. He is now charging out toward the noise, while yelling *"That's my mom"* in his language. *IT'S HAPPENING!!!!!!!!!!!*

The bond with me is unmistakable. My clients are, for the most part, forgiving of this behavior, while the dogs restrained on the scale are both surprised and curious. Steve and Lindsey are always around so there are no altercations, and Steve sets a plan into motion to suppress this unnecessary excitement.

I'm also noticing that Dexter is a little too interested in smelling the cats' post-surgery as I place them in their compartments to recover. He sniffs them initially but starts to emanate a new vocalization which I'm describing as a "dog chortle." It is a throaty guttural sound: not a bark, not a growl, more like a loud cat purr. There is no aggression and it's demonstrating what I think is his need to be involved in everything I do.

I am exposing him to the cats because we have a large black cat at home named Little Black Kitty, and I would like them to positively respond to one another. We are now witnessing a steady, slow, promising progression of Dexter's personality. His eyes aren't vacant anymore! He is starting to communicate with us.

Humans choose to have dogs for numerous reasons, but for many people, it is to give love and affection and receive it back - whether that be in the form of lying next to us, licking our hand, playing in the yard with a ball or stick, or following us around seeking our attention. We love their loyalty, their willingness to please, their companionship, and on occasion, their lack of judgment! Dexter is finally beginning to reciprocate.

It is for that reason, that we begin to plan the next steps of acclimating Dexter to his permanent residence – our home.

We do know that Dexter is very interested in our vehicle. Each day when he walks with Steve outside of the animal hospital and he passes by our car, he tugs gently on the leash to sniff the tires and doors. One can tell that he knows the pack has been inside, and he seems to have a desire to investigate the interior.

On The Inside Looking Out

-Dr. Dru Pollinger

Dexter has never shown any interest in the front windows of the animal hospital until one evening in mid-November. As we load our pack into our Ford Expedition with the usual excitement that precedes it, the headlights shine brightly on Dex's face as we pull out of the parking lot. He is now not only looking through the glass for the first time but is barking as well with a high-pitched cry. We can't believe what we are seeing! Despite the fact that I want to take him home immediately, Steve's common-sense approach dictates that we do this in a stepwise fashion. He is very emotional but maintains his pragmatism.

It is truly a roller coaster ride for me because I have looked forward to this moment for so long. Dex wants to be with us 24/7! That night at home, we discuss how to proceed – once again the "romance" for the evening is forgotten!

We have decided to bring Dexter home directly after Thanksgiving as a permanent resident. Up until now, he has been considered an illegal alien! Once a year over the Thanksgiving holiday, which is fast approaching, our entire family reunites at our home in the country.

Lots of kids, hopefully a football game... depending on how Steve's back is feeling, the Macy's Thanksgiving Day parade, and a great feast. It is a tradition we always look forward to and enjoy. This year, there is something extra to be thankful for – Dex, he is truly a miracle in progress. Being with all of us this year would be too overwhelming for Dexter, plus he has yet to ride in the car! So, before the holiday and our whole gang arrives, we decide to do a "test run."

High noon on November 20th, during our lunch break, Steve leashes Dexter and the three of us walk to the car. As the back door is opening for Dex, he lunges in and flattens himself across the entire back seat. Despite his desire to get into the car, he is not interested in looking out and remains motionless. We feel that this behavior is indicative of his need to be with us – anthropomorphism? We drive the eight miles to our home on the top of a mountain. As the house comes into view after climbing a long gravel road, the first thing that you notice is a green cyclone fence that blends into the woods bordering it. This area is an acre and a half, while the balance of the fifty acres is heavily forested with enormous boulders and rock ledges.

The sheep pasture sits behind the house and is visible through the windows inside. The front and side doors of our converted barn-style home access this fenced in front yard. Our dogs are walked daily down the road off leash, but for nighttime security from porcupines (been there, done that) and skunks, we now have peace of mind when they go out after dark.

Steve is beginning to trust Dex, but certainly not off leash, so the yard is perfect for him. He is still unpredictable with the come command, but he will allow us to leash him after a silly, playful dance.

I Am Dexter

Before we open the car doors, Steve talks to me about his plan...and he is on to something. Fingers crossed.

An Invited Guest

-Steve Pollinger

I've thought about this for quite a while and told Dru how I would proceed. I am feeling confident…and hopeful. First, Dex will walk with me at my side around the entire property for half an hour. This will let him know that he is an invited guest, not "king of the roost!" Next, I'll show him the sheep, which he may never have experienced before – but he will have to understand, as Brooklyn does so well, that I will not tolerate any predatory behavior. My energy and body language will reinforce my rules for at home behavior.

So many pet owners fail at this because they suggest to their new pet that their sanctuary is the dog's new palace – absolutely not! Aside from today, where Dex will follow my lead only, in the future he will have Brooklyn as a tutor as well. I tell Dru that I'll meet her in the house with Dexter – and ask her to "wish me luck!"

I want Dexter to inhale all the new smells and familiarize him with the sights and sounds that he will eventually become accustomed to. I open the back door of the car and begin the acclimatization. The walk around the property is uneventful. Nose to the ground, Dex sniffs this new terrain, and as expected, engages in a staring contest with ten sheep. They are as curious of him, as he is about them! They walk to the fence line, and with outstretched faces, watch him. Ernie, our big Ram, is ready to rumble with this new intruder!

I Am Dexter

Dexter begins his chortle and holds his ground. He is simply inquisitive. Half an hour later, right on schedule, I arrive back at the house with Dexter following behind.

Another Milestone

-Dr. Dru Pollinger

Dexter has taken a milestone step. He is at our home. Steve and I allow him off leash and watch him explore as we sit down in the living room area and turn on the TV to pass the time. Our first floor is entirely open aside from doors to the bedroom and bathroom. Little Black Kitty is hiding upstairs – nowhere to be seen!

The noise of the TV immediately intrigues him. How lucky can we be that a dog show is being shown on the screen? In an instant, Dex plants himself in front of this "talking box" and it is amazing to us how focused he is on this new object. It is obvious that he has never been inside a house.

Surprisingly, he begins barking at the dogs on the TV, seemingly mesmerized by their activity. The three of us sit together enjoying the interlude. We have to get back to the hospital for afternoon appointments, but Steve takes the time to show Dex the water bowl and he drinks – scents of his pack everywhere may be helping him to relax. "Mission Impossible 1" – accomplished!

We have a wonderful Thanksgiving with family, minus our pack, who remain at the animal hospital for the day. Steve and I remark after everyone leaves, that, although it would have been too much for Dex this year, next year will be different!

74

I Am Dexter

It's been not quite four months since Dexter arrived. His progress has been slow, but dogs are individuals and recover from catastrophe in their own time. Any attempt to rush their rehabilitation could have a negative effect on them. Would we both love to have him with us on the sofa? You betcha, and it will happen with time and extraordinary patience. As we write this one year later, we remember those thoughts, as he is cuddled between us!

Could It Be…A Forever Home?

-Dr. Dru Pollinger

The following Monday evening after that wonderful family Thanksgiving, Dexter becomes a permanent resident of the Pollinger household. As we leave the hospital, while it is still light, all of the dogs, including Dex, jump into the car. The fact that he clumsily hops in, unafraid, with the four other dogs, is thrilling! This is the first time we are all together in the vehicle!

Dex flattens himself in the back seat cargo area. Now, we have to deal with: the drive home, the exit from the car, the gate at the fence, Malchus' shenanigans in the yard, and the front door behavior once we arrive. The drive is uneventful. At the house, Harvey and Brooklyn get out first, and I open the gate into the yard for them. Brooklyn's excitement encourages Malchus to jump out next and seize on an opportunity to cavort with her on the front lawn. He is wildly animated, but never aggressive. If there happens to be a stick on the grass, a high energy tug of war ensues. The "old man" Chomper rushes to get out, interested only in being the first to the front door.

Dexter, who is still in the car, intently watches all of this unfold. He wants to join in but dislikes the high energy on display. He is uncomfortable seeing Malchus try to "hoink" Brooklyn, and he barks at him for the first time. Malchus has learned his lesson about fighting with Dex, so we are not concerned that there will be a skirmish. Dexter continues to bark, wanting Malchus to stop. We grab the groceries for dinner from the car and approach the front door. Dexter doesn't realize it yet…but he is entering his forever home.

I'm Here for Good!

-Dexter

This is where they must have been coming, all those dark nights when I stayed at the animal hospital. To be here with them now means that I will stay with THEM.

Is this my forever place? I feel safe with Brooklyn, Harvey, and my mom and dad.

The Routine of Home

-Dr. Dru Pollinger

There is a ritual, reinforced by Steve, in entering the house. Human first, Harvey goes next (because she is small and fast), followed by senior canine Chomper (because he is old and wise). Brooklyn and Malchus enter last. On this first night, with our new family member, and for many more to come, we invite Dexter in, but he chooses to remain outside by himself for a period of time.

We watch him from the picture window roaming around the perimeter of the yard. He sees the sheep, and this is the beginning of his acclimation to his new compound. It's approaching doggie dinner time and it is appropriate that Dexter be integrated into the process.

Steve walks outside, leashes Dexter, with some cajoling, and brings him in – so he can watch as I prepare the food. This is a crucial step for him because it is the way in which he began to connect with me at the animal hospital. However, for the first time, he will be eating with his pack. He sits quietly by the front door and watches intently as the bowls are filled. He doesn't move.

Our dinner rules are as follows: Malchus, who is always the most patient awaiting his food, has his bowl placed first, Harvey is second, Chomper third, Brooklyn fourth, and Dexter, for the time being, is last. Everyone knows the drill. They can only begin to chow down when I say the word EAT. Dexter, however, must learn this new

79

protocol. Steve sits with him until I give my command. There is no tension in the room, only the sounds of a hungry pack enjoying their dinner. We have worked very hard to establish this routine. When everyone is finished, the bowls are picked up immediately to prevent scrounging!

As Steve and I begin to prepare our own dinner, all the dogs relax on a couch except for Dexter, who lays on the living room rug. He watches us move around in the kitchen and we wonder aloud what he is thinking. The sheep are now baaaaing for their hay! So little time, so much to do!

Dexter in the wild, afraid of people. When he was finally rescued he weighed 17 pounds.

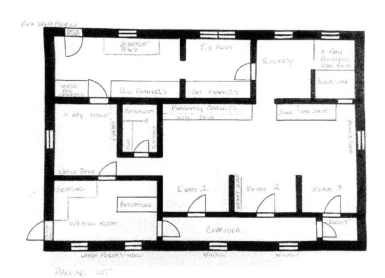

Diagram of the Pollingers' Clinic where
Dexter found his way.

Second Pond Trailhead—returning to where Dexter survived all those horrors on his own.

Top: Napping with Steve

Bottom: Dexter playing with Tony the Tiger

Top: Malchus and his pillow

Bottom: Dexter's first birthday after his rescue

Top: Plenty of room on the couch

Bottom: Annie perched on the door

Top: Steve on a pack walk

Bottom: Dexter today

Authors and rescuers

Steve and Dr. Dru Pollinger

WHITEHALL, NEW YORK

WINTER 2019

Lovin' My New Life With My Pack

-Dexter

Everything is new here but the food. I'm more nervous with all the dogs eating near me, but no one is trying to steal my dinner.

It is warm inside, and the rugs are comfortable, but I still remember fighting for scraps in the woods with the raccoons snarling and biting at me.

When the bowl was placed in front of me tonight, I was expecting that to happen. I haven't eaten with any other dogs since I was a pup, and as frightened as I am being here, I'm beginning to realize that Mom and Pop are watching out for me.

I know my name is Dexter and I know Mom feeds me well, but I'm not sure what happens next in this place.

Where will I sleep tonight – outside under a tree, inside with the other dogs? What if I have to pee? There are no urine smells in here.

There are good food smells in the air. I hear the sheep making noise outside. The wind is blowing the trees. Mom and Pop are eating at a big table. My pack is resting and now I see a big black cat at the top of the stairs! Will watch and wait. That is what I do best.

Now, why are they getting up and cleaning all the dishes? I'll be hungry again real soon. After a time, Mom and Pop sit down on the sofas with the other dogs and turn on the TV – I remember this from when I came here alone, once before. We all lie around until I hear Pop say, "Dru, I think it's time to walk them." He gets up first, puts on his jacket and Mom does the same.

The dogs look eager and Pop says to Mom, "Let's try to keep the energy level as low as possible – at least tonight." Malchus and I are leashed, and Pop goes out the door first, with the two of us behind. As Mom approaches, little Harvey scurries by us and Chomper and Brooklyn are called outside. Everyone seems to know what to do!

What is next? Pop opens the gate, and we begin our pack walk down a dirt road. I hear myself beginning to howl because I am scared of the woods on either side. It reminds me of where I was trapped. It is different here from the sidewalks at the animal hospital that I got used to – knowing that we would return safely to my shelter. Dad bends down and while hugging me, strokes my chest. This momentary reassurance helps me, but it does not override my fear.

We walk for twenty minutes, everyone smelling, pooping, and peeing. I continue to be nervous and I bark intermittently to let everyone know how I feel. Brooklyn stays close to me which helps.

Everyone else is interested in the smells. I am a bit distracted by the scent of a fox but continue to walk along at Pop's side with Malchus, who is fascinated with everything and is beginning to show high energy. They all seem secure and so I finally stop to pee, and Mom congratulates me!

It's beginning to get dark, as we do an about face and walk back the way we came. Are we going to the car, the house, or are we staying outside? As we approach the fenced in yard, Pop ignores the car, opens the gate and we're back inside. What if I have to pee again? Mom says to Pop "Let's relax and see how things play out."

Pop sprawls out on the sofa, leaving enough room for Brooklyn, who always loves to be near him. Mom sits on the other sofa with Harvey in her lap. Malchus lies next to her and puts his head on her leg. Chomper lays down in the kitchen, where the floor is cool. I need to watch and learn how this unfamiliar environment works for me. I sit on the floor, ten feet away – able to see what everyone is doing at a glance. I am near enough to be a part of the pack, but far enough away to run, if I need to.

Middle of the Night Antics

-Dr. Dru Pollinger

Steve and I turn on some soft music and finally have a chance to relax. It's been a tough day at the animal hospital pulling porcupine quills and stabilizing a dog that was hit by a car, on top of plowing through routine appointments. The anticipation of wondering how Dexter will do at home with us has knocked us out. Steve literally hobbles to the bathroom and I am left alone for a few minutes to contemplate how Dexter will handle his peeing problem overnight.

The medication he is on certainly helps to control his urination during the day, when he can go in and out. But he is not capable yet of communicating to us any desire to go outside in the middle of the night and relieve himself if an urge occurs.

When he slept at the hospital, we would always have to clean up overnight accidents. As Steve heads to the bedroom, he optimistically says that, maybe Dex will follow Brooklyn's lead, when she goes out during the night. I smile to myself, knowing that all of the dogs have a way of alerting ME, while I'm sleeping, of their desire to go outside, if necessary. Hopefully, Steve is right! He is the one who sleeps soundly, while I am an insomniac, always awakening to the slightest noise.

We guessed wrong! When we get up to make a pot of coffee in the morning, we see a puddle next to the club chair by the door. Although I had gotten up several times during the night, Dexter had

94

not shown any indication of wanting to go outside. Lysol spray and some paper towels solve the problem, for now. It was his first night, and we agree that with time and patience (our new mantra), he will learn to follow the pack in their overnight behavior.

For the next six weeks, we become accustomed to Dexter peeing in that same spot... *and only that spot*, overnight. Despite the fact that I encourage him to go out with Brooklyn, who awakens me by whining, the behavior continues. We put down pads to protect the floor, I increase his medication dose, I encourage him to follow Brooklyn and Chomper outside – all to no avail! Potty training puppies is a much easier process, but we are dealing with an adult dog that has a medical problem and has never been housetrained!

Dexter has become more relaxed with our nightly routine and has acclimated fairly well. We've had a decent amount of snow and he has been spending less time outdoors and wanting to come inside and be comfortable with his family. He sleeps on the rug in the living room at night, by choice, while Brooklyn and the other dogs switch back and forth between the bed and the carpet in our bedroom. During the day, Dexter stays with our pack in the office and living room at the animal hospital. He avoids having accidents by going in and out with them. Steve is consulting with some professional friends about Dexter's nocturia.

Too many opinions, no results, and continued frustration push him to find his own answer! Because of the long walks that he has with Dexter on a daily basis, he notices over time that Dex's eyes are now continually focused on him. Steve not only relishes this behavior but decides to utilize this wonderful attribute.

It's 2:30 am, toward the end of January, and shockingly, Steve gets up, puts on his pants and a T- shirt. No slippers, no sneakers – he walks into the living room, opens the front door, and begins to sneak outside, calling softly to Dexter. As I awaken and ask him what's going on, he gives me the "shhhhh" sign with his finger to his lips.

As Dexter follows him, I look out the window and watch my husband pee on a large tree near the porch. I'm in disbelief, because I know how grumpy Steve is when he awakens in the middle of the night.

Sure enough, Dexter follows suit. Steve bends down in the snow, congratulates Dexter verbally, and hugs him. It is fifteen degrees outside and I'm beginning to think that my husband is losing it, until I see him reach into his pocket and reward the dog with a piece of liverwurst. I also realize that the plastic Ziploc™ bag in his pants pocket was creating the odor I had been noticing for several days. Another hug for Dex, and as he marches in with the dog, I see the big grin on his face! "Are you losing it, Steve?" and he replies, "*No, baby, give me a week, and this problem will be solved!*" Steve is acting like a peacock! The other dogs did not follow Dexter outside and look at him like he's crazy. "*Hey, sweetie, since we're both up?!!!*"

Dexter Finds His Voice

-Dr. Dru Pollinger

Up until now, the only barking that Dexter has done is at Malchus, when he chases Brooklyn in the yard to "hoink" her. "Hoinking" is the word we chose to use when the kids were small, and they asked questions about one dog being on top of another! I'm getting a little frustrated that Steve hasn't corrected Malchus' energy yet. However, it is difficult when we come home at night to unload five dogs, who are anticipating dinner, along with groceries and various sundries. The sheep also expect to be fed at this time, and we're hungry too, and tired. We do our best to control the situation, but maybe not so professionally.

One night, in the beginning of February, when I was particularly stressed out and overtired, I awoke from a dream, or what I thought was a dream – to a new noise. It was a loud demanding bark, and I wasn't even sure it was real, until I heard it again – even louder. I walked into the living room and there was Dexter, sitting at the front door, yelling at it to open for him!

I was in utter disbelief and ran over to let him out. He raced down the steps and as I turned on the porch light, I could see him peeing on Steve's tree in the snow!! It had been four days since Steve started his nighttime ritual with Dexter and the liverwurst. So far, Dexter had not peed again on the club chair. Hallelujah! Steve is still fast asleep. I imagine all the dogs are applauding for Dex. I go to the fridge and reward him with some liverwurst.

From this night on, the accidents cease, and Dexter no longer looks for a treat. However, for the next two evenings, my husband continues to repeat his nightly routine, forgetting that the problem is solved!

Dexter has found his voice and is now able to communicate his every desire to us. He barks to go out, he barks for his dinner, he barks for his medicine rolled up in peanut butter, and he barks for Brooklyn to join him outside. He barks to alert us when a car drives up the driveway. He barks at the sheep baaaing in the pasture. He barks when he hears the coy dogs, and he barks at other dogs that he sees through the car window. Now, the rest of our pack is barking when Dexter barks!!!

I Am Dexter

-Dexter

I am Dexter. I know now how to get what I want, and I know this is helping me to move up in the pack hierarchy.

I can talk, and Mom and Pop listen. I am beginning to enjoy my new life and the comforts that come with having a home. I still have fears, but when I'm walking at Pop's side, I am less afraid than I used to be.

The sheep still bother me – they are big and hang out together. I worry when Mom and Pop go out in the pasture and they run toward them making their baaaa noises. I am not allowed near them because I bark, and they get spooked.

Hopefully, when the snow is gone, I can go in with them and figure them out. Just when I think I have all of my ducks in a row, there is a new arrival!

A Funny Feline Frenzy

-Dr. Dru Pollinger

Our older white cat named Crash had died suddenly in his sleep, prior to Dexter coming home with us. He and Little Black Kitty (who grew into a big black cat – even bigger than Harvey), had been inseparable.

When Crash was gone, Little Black Kitty began hiding upstairs during the day, coming down only for dinner. I had to go to the second floor to engage him in play, and I soon realized that he needed another feline friend. Steve, who is not particularly a cat person, surprised me in early March with a little black and white kitten that needed a home. Her mother had died shortly after giving birth and the owner was destitute. She asked us to please take the kitten, as she had no means to care for it.

Steve has a big heart and knows this was the right fix for Little Black Kitty, who was extremely lonely. We watched the new kitty at the hospital for a few days after vaccinating her and addressing her medical needs and recognized immediately that she was a wild woman and could hold her own!

We named her Annie and brought her home to see how she would interact with all our animals. This three-and-a-half-pound fur-ball, dotted with speckles and blotches, entered the house in a cat carrier and was placed on a table in the living room for all the dogs to

100

see. Little Black Kitty remained at the top of the stairs, frozen in place, as he listened to the soft meows coming from her plastic box. I opened the carrier and she immediately emerged, anxious to scope out her new surroundings.

Dexter was instantly on alert – a little too much so! He began to make his chortle noise and Steve corrected him immediately. This was the first time that Steve used his touch to distract and dissuade Dex's behavior. It worked – the chortle stopped, and Steve now held the kitten in the palm of his hand for Dexter to smell. I knew from Dex's prior cat introductions at the animal hospital that he would not be aggressive. The kitten was unafraid, and Dexter sat down to observe.

The rest of the dogs were used to multiple cats in the house and seemed disinterested for approximately five minutes. We might as well have taken in a squirrel, a rabbit, or a chipmunk, because this kitten was lightning fast and crazy. She immediately began to explore every nook and cranny and catapulted herself from one piece of furniture to the next.

Steve's Saturday afternoon siesta was interrupted, and he was filled with …shall we say, negative energy? She knocked off several of his antique dog trophies on top of the fireplace, and as far as our dogs were concerned, the race was on to catch up with her. This was the first time Brooklyn was disobedient and Steve went wild.

As he got up from the sofa, attempting to control the chaos, he knocked over his coffee mug and tripped on the rug. Now he's after everybody, including me, for bringing the cat home! He made DeNiro's acting in Goodfellows look like a cartoon, and of course, he conveniently forgot that he was the one that okayed the kitten to begin with.

Annie discovered within minutes that the dogs couldn't reach her on top of the door. From her high up perch, she gave everyone the finger and settled in for the afternoon.

I simply maintained my calm state, trying not to laugh, knowing that everything always works out in the end – doesn't it?

As the winter blues descended upon us, Annie kept us amused at home, to say it politely. The dogs did learn to accept her presence and she became Little Black Kitty's amigo, which was the original purpose of the adoption. She learned the art of surprise and the gift of speed and found it impossible to leave the dogs alone. Their wagging tails were of particular interest to her – most of all, Dexter's. He began to sleep with one eye open. She truly enjoyed our 200-year-old post and beam barn house, thinking that the wooden perches were made expressly for her!

Feeling More at Home Every Day

-Dexter

I guess I will have to submit to this fast-moving blob of fur, constantly invading my space. Mom and Pop rule.

At least she goes upstairs at night and I have some peace. I'm sleeping most nights on the sofa now, but I'm starting to enjoy the comfort of the bed when I see an open spot.

I wag my tail now whenever my name is called, and I know my name is Dexter. I do not enjoy the frigid winter weather – it is a continual reminder of my life before.

RANGELEY, MAINE

SPRING 2019

The Maine Event

-Dr. Dru Pollinger

Ten years ago, we recognized the need for a weekend retreat from an extremely busy workload at the hospital – which we say with pride. Having a pack of dogs always with us limited the ability to travel in well-populated urban areas.

An old friend and well-known artist had been encouraging us to visit a small town in western Maine called Rangeley – population year-round of 1,100. The fact that Dave knew our work ethic and time constraints so well, prompted him to suggest that Steve learn to fly fish for relaxation in this beautiful area.

The locale is world- renowned because of President Eisenhower's fishing trips to this region and the difficulty for the Secret Service to oversee his complete protection! This densely forested terrain, home to over five hundred natural ponds and lakes, makes the Adirondacks, where Dex hailed from, look sparse in comparison.

The last hour of a four-and-a-half-hour trip would afford us something special. An abundance of moose crisscrossing the county routes, as well as the occasional fox, bobcat, bear, and numerous deer, always made the trip exciting and enjoyable.

So, after several investigatory sojourns, we invested in a small summer cabin, in dire need of a makeover, directly (meaning seventy-five feet away) on Quimby Pond.

This small fly-fishing haven prohibited motorized boats, which made it a perfect place for our dogs to romp and swim. Direct access to an extensive trail system was virtually a stone's throw away. Pre-Dexter, we were able to get away for a long weekend twice a month during the spring, summer, and fall.

Steve spent the majority of his time redoing the cabin, and to this day has still not learned to fly fish! The dogs, however, have a wonderful time. "Queen Bee" Brooklyn swims with the ducks and loons, peacefully enjoying the exercise, while the other dogs wade at the water's edge.

Our dog pack has changed over the years from Scottish Deerhounds and old Goldens to our current pack, which is far more diversified! Again, the area is so remote that we were fortunate enough to have a bull moose peering in our window early one Saturday morning, defying the fenced in barking dogs alerting us to his presence!

After acquiring Dexter and working so hard to rehabilitate him, we were unable to make the trip to Maine for many months. But in May of 2019, we felt confident enough to bring him with us, knowing with certainty that he would enjoy the long car ride, but unsure how he might interact in his new environs.

On May 15, 2019, we set out on a sunny Thursday morning, beginning a new journey with Dexter. Our typical stops included the Woodstock Market, where we stocked up on good eats for the weekend, and a pit stop in White River Junction. There, we walked the dogs near a bank complex. This parking lot bordered a hotel and children's day care center and had a large grassy field where our pack could sniff and pee.

From there, we drove to Lancaster, New Hampshire – about an hour and a half further. Steve, having some fun along the way, always visits the consignment shop where he peruses the free clothing rack, choosing new outdated outfits for Lindsey (as a joke). We enjoy her laughter on our return, knowing she will never appear in these recycled clothes.

We exercised the dogs once again at the Fairgrounds, with all new smells for Dexter. It becomes evident that new experiences for him are accompanied by incessant barking episodes which, at first, we don't understand the meaning of. He is great in the car, but we soon realize that "newness" in his mind is a threat to the pack and he is making "noise" to alert them of possible danger. Affecting no one but us, with his loud vocalization, we decide to let it play out. The other dogs remain calm.

We gas up in a town called Erroll in New Hampshire and make a turn onto Route 16, the last leg of the journey and the most enjoyable part of the ride for us. This is where it becomes truly rural America, and the wildlife abounds.

Driving this road has an element of danger, because it is here that the moose unexpectedly pop out of the woods on either side. There are numerous "Brake for Moose" signs. Hitting a moose can cause fatalities, so drivers typically slow down a bit and are constantly on alert. Depending on the time of day and season of the year, one might see several or none of these beasts.

The back windows are down a bit as the weather is pleasant, and our hound dog's nose picks up the scent of a roadside moose before we even see him. Dexter is wide-eyed and barking. As he hails from the Adirondacks, we don't know if this is his first moose encounter. We slow down and enjoy the temporary presence of this majestic animal. As she lumbers off into the pine trees, the other dogs remain relatively calm, knowing Steve's attitude toward uncontrollable behavior, which they respect.

It is always a pleasurable experience to witness a moose in a natural environment as opposed to seeing one in a refuge. The last half hour of the trip is uneventful until we make the sharp hairpin turn onto the gravel road leading to the camp.

This is the only time Steve allows Brooklyn to show her uncontrollable excitement. We know that upon pulling into our driveway, she will fly out the open car door, race to the dock, and dive as far as she can into the water. She loves to swim, and what is more remarkable is that the curious ducks paddle toward her. Her dog mentality of "live and let live" is ever present, for she shows absolutely no aggression.

Dexter, who always looks toward her for guidance, is a bit bewildered. He begins barking but is embracing this new experience and observing the other dogs as well. He is torn between watching the excited pack and taking in the smells!

We do not feel comfortable enough letting him off leash with the other dogs. Always cognizant of his horrendous past, we are vigilant about keeping him leashed. We are determined to understand more about dogs with PTS and the triggers that could possibly revive it. He will be well taken care of this weekend, with lots of long walks and hopefully smells that are new and exciting for him. A half hour passes quickly, and it is time to unpack the car and introduce Dexter to the cabin.

Always, and I mean always…security comes first, and so upon purchasing this cabin a decade ago, a backyard, green cyclone fence was installed for the dog's enjoyment and our peace of mind! We would never choose to live in a gated community like Tomac's "Villages" (a community in Florida where Steve's childhood friend lives), but our dogs must. We now show Dexter his new backyard play area in Maine.

As Dex explores his new yard with his cohorts, Steve and I watch Brooklyn dock dive and reminisce about a family contest the year before. Brooklyn's competitive drive is phenomenal, but not witnessed by anyone but us.

When a ball or stick is thrown anywhere, this nine-year-old Pitbull will be the first to retrieve it and bring it back to us. She will steal the ball from another dog using tactical maneuvers like a great football player. Having this secret knowledge, Steve accepted a sucker bet with our son Brett on a preplanned family weekend in the summer of 2018 (prior to acquiring Dexter), when we were at Quimby Pond with our pack.

Brett visited Rangeley with his wife Marissa, baby girl Leah and his three labs, renting a cabin on a lake near ours. He challenged Steve and Brooklyn to a dock diving and stick retrieval contest with his best swimming dog, Melania. He was to prepare the area for the "event" at his cabin – obviously thinking his dog would have the edge. The bet was for a $200 dinner in Rangeley that evening.

Remember the chapter about younger Steve and his tenacity? As the witching hour approached, Steve asked me to drive while he sat in the back seat with Brooklyn. The rest of the canine entourage were in the cargo area, ready to cheer her on. My husband coached Brooklyn by talking in her ear much like a boxing coach would do with their fighter in the corner. The enjoyment for me is watching the father and son try and outsmart one another. Arriving at their cabin, Brooklyn's energy, to please Steve, rose to an eleven on a one to ten scale!

He opened the car door and as she raced down to the dock, Steve witnessed the color draining out of Brett's face. In his typical sneaky style, my son threw the stick early, giving his Lab, Melania, the lead. Steve yells to me, "No worries" when Melania grabs the stick in the water as Brooklyn takes her dive.

Our raging Pitbull soars through the air and in seconds grabs the stick from Melania's mouth and returns it to shore. Steve is overcome with gloating and decides to make a quick exit to reward Brooklyn with a hamburger.

I remained on the edge of the pond listening to the neighbors who rented the house to Brett and Marissa. They witnessed the whole scene, but not quite understanding what was going on, they seemed more interested in whether their screened in porch might be destroyed by the other two Labs cavorting around, anxious to participate in the festivities!

A year later as we laugh about "the contest," we wonder if down the road Dexter will match his mentor Brooklyn. We will see.

The Cabin…First Visit

-Dr. Dru Pollinger

I unlock the back door to the cabin, anxious to watch Dex investigate. Steve calls Brooklyn in from her glorious swim and we prepare for the evening. We light a fire in the woodstove to warm the living room-kitchen area, and Steve stretches out on the La-Z-Boy. I fill a bowl of water for the dogs, who are always thirsty after the long ride.

The first thing Dexter does is walk the cabin, sniffing as he goes. Seeing Harvey jump on the sofa, he follows suit and makes himself comfortable. He seems outwardly at ease.

Steve and I check in with Lindsey at the animal hospital, make the necessary calls, and look forward to a good meal – one that I can take my time to prepare. Good smells fill the cabin, and we eat, watching TV.

My Road Trip to Maine

-Dexter

I love the ride in the car, and my new yard smells interesting. Will I be left here? I'm always worried that the good stuff will end.

Why are we in this place? What's for dinner? Where are the cats? I'm anxious, but I sense that everyone is relaxed. The fire is nice and Pop turns on the TV. Mom is busy in the kitchen.

As usual, I watch and wait for what is next. I hear a car passing by the driveway – is someone coming for me? The tire sounds go away. Next time, I'll bark and alert the pack. I smell dinner, and as usual, I'm starving. The bowls are placed, Mom says EAT and I forget about everything else!

I have to pee – I bark sharply to let everyone know. Mom and Pop applaud me with a "good boy" and I'm outside in a flash. No sheep here to bark at, but the chipmunks are chattering at my presence. Now, I hear quacking sounds coming from the water. I've seen these ducks before – in my long-ago time.

113

They don't bother me. Everyone follows me into the yard and Malchus is starting with Brooklyn again. Mom and Pop have leashes and we line up at the gate. There are no sidewalks here – it's a little bit like home and I know a good walk is coming.

As we leave the driveway and start down a dirt road, I see people on bikes coming toward us – bikes, I know from my walks at the animal hospital. They talk to Mom and Pop and ask questions about the new dog – that must be me, because they know everyone else's name. Pop says, "You can pet him." I'm afraid of this new hand coming toward me, but I allow it, and surprisingly it feels good. Too much chit chat, and I tug on my leash to let Pop know it's time to get a move on.

"Brooklyn, how do Mom and Pop know all of these people? They don't sniff each other's butts, and yet they are trusting. I'm not fearful up here, because Mom and Dad are with us all the time.

I like the longer leash on the hikes because I can explore more. When do you think Dad will let me run free, like the rest of you? I'll stay with everybody because that's where I feel safe. Dad's not trusting me yet, even though I'm coming to him whenever he calls. I hope it's soon. The new smells are calling!"

A Great Day With More to Come

-Steve Pollinger

Dusk is approaching, and we head back to our warm camp, ready to settle in for the night. Dexter immediately hops on the bed in the back room, to secure a spot, even though everyone else is in the living room watching TV. Later on, as I begin turning off the lights, Dexter runs to the back door anticipating one more pee, and the pack follows him out. We are all exhausted from the long drive, and our first night is uneventful. We fall asleep to the sound of the loons on the pond.

The sun is up, and Dex is the first one up barking at the door to go out. We're very proud of him for recognizing that peeing is only outside. My morning routine when we are at the cabin, is to drive into town to pick up Dru's favorite cinnamon rolls and coffee. I always takes one or two dogs, and this morning I chose Dexter, who is eager to ride in the car. Today, however, Dex clumsily jumps into the empty front passenger seat. He is riding shotgun this morning!

Donuts and My Dad

-Dexter

We're going somewhere – just Pop and me, and I like looking out the big front window. When we stop, after a short ride, Pop leaves the car windows down a little. Now, I can watch him as he leaves me, and I can sniff the air which is filled with delicious donut smells – my favorite, next to liverwurst. I'm exercising my voice to remind him to come back. When he finally comes out, carrying a bag, and sits down behind the wheel, I relax. To my delight, he offers me a small piece of something new from the bag. I wag and stare for more. One more piece for me, he says and the bag closes.

Rangeley Retreat

-Steve Pollinger

Back at the cabin, we enjoy our simple breakfast and get ready for a long hike in the woods. This is why we come here! The vast forested area surrounding the cabins on the pond is interrupted by miles of snowmobile trails. We begin our walk down the dirt access road and veer off on a familiar path which takes us deep into the woods. I reward Brooklyn's good behavior and allow her off leash along with old man Chomper and Harvey. As usual, Dexter is "connected at the hip to me" (as Dru would say), because his nose knows no boundaries here. Malchus is a little unpredictable in these surroundings, and Dru walks him at her side. I have a heavy stick - which I hold in my hand, to ward off evil spirits! We do not own a gun but need some form of protection!

This Place Isn't Bad at All

-Dexter

Everywhere I look, I see my pack pooping and peeing. Malchus makes it a big deal, circling to find just the right spot. Harvey is very discreet – "wham, bam, thank you mam." Chomper stops in the center of the path, in a sitting position, and is done. Everyone anticipates Brooklyn's poop – for some reason, it smells the best, and we all watch and sniff it out. I am last because I like to do my business with something tickling my butt. It can be a pine tree branch or a low-lying shrub, or some tall, thick grass. I do a short dance, give a quick grunt, and am now relieved of my load.

Mom and Pop are excited, because to them, there will be fewer clean-ups in the backyard. As I am relaxed, walking next to Pop, I find myself thinking, as I do on occasion, when all seems good. Earlier, when we were back at the cabin eating breakfast pastry tidbits, Dad came over to me on the sofa and put his arms around my body.

I was nervous – I don't quite understand this behavior although I watch him do it to everyone else – including Mom. I jumped off the couch to get away and I could feel his energy change – I know he wanted a different outcome.

I loved the long walk in the woods, particularly knowing I am safe, with Mom, Dad, and the pack. I'm tired when we get back to our fenced in yard, and I lie down in the sun. Dad takes out a machine that eats the grass and makes it smooth for us. He starts walking back and forth in front of me. Malchus doesn't like the noise, but it doesn't bother me.

I hear Mom yelling "lunchtime," and we all follow Pop in, through the cabin and out onto the front deck. I see a feast on the outdoor table, and it smells really good, but I know from past reprimands, that I am not included in this meal!

Better for me to lie down, watch, and wait for Pop to give me a treat. There's a new routine up here; we are all together, all the time. We go for another short hike after which, Mom and Dad relax on the sofa.

They are talking a lot, and Mom is writing. Why does she keep saying my name aloud? I'm sleepy now.

I'll go lie down with Brooklyn on the bed. When I come back out – everyone is sleeping. I know it's close to dinnertime. I bark to wake everyone up, and it works.

Tonight's dinner tastes really good – maybe that's what is special about this new place. When it's dark, Mom and Pop take a shower and get dressed all over again. Now I watch them leave the cabin without us. No one else seems to mind, so I will stare at the back door and wait. I can smell where they are going – it's not that far away. I hear their voices at the house next door – those people have that crazy Lab that loves to swim, like Brooklyn. I had a really fun time here...I hope we come back again.

Steve & Dr. Dru Pollinger

RANGELEY, MAINE

SUMMER 2019

The Dog Days of Our Summer

- Dru Pollinger

Our long weekend in Maine was enjoyable, as always. It is hard to drive back home and face reality, but we are thinking about the wonderful time we had introducing Dexter to our magical getaway. We are witnessing his transition to becoming a family pet and a welcome addition to a close-knit pack.

Our summer routine revolves around work and home activities. We are constantly reinforcing a regimen for Dexter that helps build his self- confidence. He is no longer looking for escape routes and wants to be present with us, wherever we are.

His eyes are softer now. The dark irises, the color of Hershey's chocolate, are more visible. His pupils are no longer in a state of perpetual dilation. For the most part, he is relaxed when he stares, always watching what is transpiring before him. He has knowledge of who we are and what we mean to him. The tail wags when we return his look. His repose is peaceful. His quiet breathing reassures us that he is content. The invisible wounds are healing. From the beginning, we saw a desire in this dog to love and be loved.

It's the end of July, and we've enjoyed several more long weekends with the pack up in Maine. Steve has put Dexter on a fifteen-foot leash, to allow him to frolic at the water's edge.

We know now that he hasn't swam before, because he is reluctant to go out as far as Brooklyn does. He enjoys watching the kayakers go by, and Steve spells out his name verbally, to a couple in a canoe – suggesting they call him out into the water, but he is not interested in swimming. The bottom of the pond is too rocky and slippery, so we will have to find a better lake substrate to walk him on, while teaching him to swim.

Years ago, we taught Chomper to swim, at a cement boat launch, on the way up to Maine. We tossed a tennis ball farther and farther into the water, until he was successfully swimming out to grab and retrieve the toy. He is as good a swimmer as Brooklyn, just slower, due to his age. Dexter, however, does not play fetch!

We will adjust our strategy and make sure he enjoys the water also. His pack behavior has become normalized, and he is now barking and alerting everyone, to passing vehicles, bikers, people walking, and other dogs coming down the road behind the cabin.

WHITEHALL, NY & FAIR HAVEN, VT

SUMMER 2019

Feeling Safer Every Day

-Dexter

The weather seems to be getting warmer and warmer and I'm remembering a long time ago, when I was living in the woods, how all of a sudden – I wasn't cold anymore. This day was uneventful with nice leash walks and I had a good dinner, as usual.

Mom and Pop are going to bed early. I have seen them do this before, when they are working very hard at the animal hospital. Tonight, I decide to come in timely when Mom opens the back door (usually I like to stay outside longer than the rest of my pack). I run in, jump on the bed, and take up the bottom middle half as always. I love this bed! CRASH, BANG and then again!! Is someone trying to break in?

Mom tries to settle me and says, "It is only a thunderstorm." Still nervous, my body finds its way to the top of the bed, in between my Pop and my Mom. Being up in the middle is calming and reassuring, particularly since Mom put her arm around me.

Birthday Bandana

-Dexter

It's August 1, 2019, and I just came back from my morning walk at the animal hospital and Pop is in a fun mood – a little unusual for him this early in the day.

The UPS truck came and dropped off a small package. He's excited as he rips open the box. He smiles at this silly little rag and shows it to Lindsey. As she laughs hysterically, he explains to her that it's a bandana (whatever that is) for my birthday celebration and he shows her the words "HAPPY BIRTHDAY."

I hear him say "Now, Lindsey, next Tuesday, August 6, 2019, is designated as Dexter's "first official" birthday. We will have had him for 1 year!" I heard my name, but I don't understand any of the other words. Pop says he's going to put the rag around my neck and Malchus, Chomper, Brooklyn and Harvey will have birthday hats. Lindsey offers to make doggie pupcakes the night before and Mom announces that on the big day, everyone has to sing to me.

What does one year mean? It seems to mean a lot to my family. Are they giving me away? Am I going somewhere new? Do they still want me? Earlier this morning, before my walk, Pop picked me up and put me on the moving weight table in the hospital. I was terrified as usual, but he seemed pleased with the number "60." My fear made me empty my anal glands and Mom had to clean it up – Pop always stays away from the messy stuff. She was happy with the number because she said it meant that my new food was working. I like being fat. I can't wait for the birthday food!

A Doggone Great Party

-Dr. Dru Pollinger

It's early in the morning on Dexter's special day, and one by one, we bring our pack into the reception area. Brooklyn loves her party hat and starts dancing around wagging her tail, thinking all the attention is for her. Harvey's head is too small for her hat, so we allow her to go naked. Chomper, as usual, is very accepting of his head gear, and Malchus, our "clown dog," looks silly with one half ear!

"Okay, Steve, I say, it's time for Dexter, and we'll start to sing as you come through the door. I want to film this, so I can send it on to Florence."

As Steve opens the door and Dexter follows him in, his dogface appears overwhelmed, and a new shyness comes over him that we haven't witnessed before. He has heard me sing in the past, but now everyone is singing the birthday song, and it is directed at him. He sits and stares at all the dogs with their hats and excited energy, while his new HAPPY BIRTHDAY bandana sparkles around his neck.

We didn't feel that he would accept a party hat on his head – maybe next year. Lindsey is frosting her pupcakes at the front desk, while enjoying the festivities, and now all the dogs are sniffing the air. Without further ado, everyone pushes to get to Lindsey first, which Brooklyn easily accomplishes, and she is now walking around with cream cheese icing on her nose! Dexter observes for a minute or two

129

and then decides it is his turn. He gently takes his pupcake and now everyone is snacking, including me! They are delicious!

It's hard to imagine that we have had Dexter for an entire year, and we reminisce about his progress. Here we are, sitting together in the same reception area that so terrified him a year ago. He now sees the entire complex as his, which is exactly what we had hoped for. As the doggie excitement winds down, Steve instructs Lindsey to hand out any remaining pupcakes to our client's dogs over the course of the day. Now we review the video and all enjoy a good laugh! I send it on to Florence, so that she can feel a part of this wonderful celebration. She calls later on to thank us and wish Dexter the best.

A Reunion With Coyote Trapper Mark Laske

-Dr. Dru Pollinger

In mid-August of 2019, Steve was able to contact Mark Laske, the wildlife rehabilitator who lived in North Creek, New York. He invited Mark to meet us at the animal hospital to reunite with Dexter.

I was very excited to come face to face with him, as I had not been present in the waiting room when Dexter first arrived. I had many questions to ask! He was anxious to see how Dex was doing and made the two hour journey several days after the call.

Tuesday, August 20th was a beautiful day. Mark parked his vehicle on the front lawn under the big maple tree, so that his new dog – an 8-year-old rescue, would be comfortable in the shade. Steve brought Dexter out on a leash and sat down on the front steps, with Dex on his right side. He then invited Mark to sit next to Dex, so that the dog remained in the middle.

Mark was able to slowly put his arm around Dexter and interact with him in a normal way! He was overjoyed and I took a photo so he could remember this moment. Did Dexter remember Mark? Probably not, but because he trusted Steve, he allowed this good touch from someone new.

Mark spoke with me for several hours, mainly about Dexter, but also about his experiences as a wildlife rehabilitator at the Adirondack

131

Wildlife Refuge. He had resigned from that position right around the time that Dex was captured.

As one can imagine, there were many amazing stories about his interactions with birds and animals, particularly wolves. I was impressed by his wealth of knowledge and enjoyed our conversation.

My first question for him was how Dex got his name? It turns out that after he was trapped, he was taken to the veterinary hospital in Shroon Lake the following day.

At the reception desk, Mark had to come up with a name for the intake form. He wrote "DX," which in medical terms, (Mark was a male nurse prior to his wildlife job), is short for "diagnosis" The receptionist/technician inadvertently entered the name as DEX, not realizing that she had now given him his forever moniker!

We then talked about what he knew, if anything, of Dexter's past. He recounted that he had first seen a picture of the emaciated dog mid-winter, on a New York Ski Blog site, online.

A man had seen this "lost dog" once, took a photo, and wrote about his encounter. Mark also knew about the people (including the cook) feeding him at Garnet Hill Lodge, and that one of the caretakers there figured he would just let the dog hang around.

The dog catcher had wanted to shoot him, "but not with kids around," and told people not to feed him – that he would give them tickets! I will not name names. You should know Steve by now, and he wanted to shoot the dog catcher! There were also several attempts by others to catch him to have him euthanized. Mark heard stories about Dex stealing eggs from the roadside kiosks of local poultry farms – he would actually grab a full egg carton and take off with it into the woods!

Dexter was also discussed on NEWS10 ABC's Pet Connection, which always included segments on lost pets as well as Humane Society adoptions. We attempted to contact the station numerous times. It was disappointing that they never responded to our inquiries.

For the time that Dexter stayed at Mark's place, he had shelter, was well fed, and even introduced to another dog named Cooper – a well-mannered golden retriever. The first visit went okay but by the second visit, Dex was "grumbly," according to Mark. He spent most of his time in an outdoor, fenced in enclosure, but had access to a garage area with a kennel.

Mark did notice that he drank a lot of water and peed excessively. He tried to get him to come inside his home, but although Dex cautiously entered on several occasions, enticed by food, he chose to remain outside at a distance.

In conversations with Florence, Mark expressed his desire to keep Dex, if he could get him inside the house before October 1st and the coming winter.

In his last conversation with her, he said that he was not being successful with the rehabilitation in a timely fashion, and that waiting longer was not a good plan. As fate would have it, Florence reached out to Steve and the meeting to transfer Dex was scheduled.

After our meeting with Mark, who generously gave us his time, we sent him a framed photo. In the picture, he has his arm wrapped around Dexter. He replied to us in an email: "Yes, got the pic, awesome, can't believe he was just leaning up against me with my arm around him…you guys are truly life savers!"

Dexter – the Patient

-Dr. Dru Pollinger

Survivors such as Dex don't necessarily bemoan their fate. The Holocaust survivors that came to America attempted to move forward – outwardly, at least. This dog faced at least six hard months in the remote woods, often without food, while battling nature's predators. He suffered both psychological and physical wounds.

First, we've been addressing his severe mental trauma, but now, a year later, we will have to anesthetize him to correct severe periodontal disease and a right rear foot issue that has worsened over time.

General anesthesia is a stepwise process. An initial intramuscular injection of certain drugs makes dogs sleepy and enables an intravenous catheter to be easily placed, usually in a front leg vein.

Following this, an intravenous injection is given that causes a temporary relaxed sleepy state. Intubation, where an endotracheal tube is placed in the trachea, proceeds, whereupon gas anesthesia can begin. There are always risks associated with anesthetizing an animal, despite the fact that they are carefully monitored throughout this process. I feel comfortable and competent in my ability to perform surgical procedures on my own animals.

Others may feel differently. Steve would have nothing done if I weren't the one doing it, although if something is beyond my expertise,

I will certainly refer it. He is very aware of the medical complications that can ensue from even simple operations.

Now it is imperative to move forward. My husband does insist that Brooklyn be with Dexter throughout the day. She can give him a psychological lift and is the right match for a blood donor – God forbid!

The night before the planned procedure, Steve gets no sleep. He is so bonded with this dog that he worries incessantly about something going wrong. At 4:00 am he gets up and drives to the animal hospital to check on the amount of oxygen in the tank – despite it being filled three days before! Fresh hot coffee and a second shower in six hours do nothing to placate his anxiety! This is normal behavior for him when he has something on his mind, so I am not troubled. I can go back to sleep. Dexter is sprawled out in his usual spot at the bottom of the bed, oblivious to everything going on around him.

Surgery Day

-Dr. Dru Pollinger

Steve can read Dex and Dex can now read Steve! His typical positive energy is off, and the dog senses this as he walks through the door of the animal hospital.

Lindsey is directed to lock the front door, put up the "EMERGENCY SURGERY" sign, and switch the phone to voicemail only. Steve will have to restrain Dexter for the first injection, and he decides to have him sit on the comfortable sofa next to Brooklyn while I do this. He holds Dex more tenderly than I have ever seen him do for our five children! Step one is completed.

Twenty minutes later, we carry our sleepy dog to the surgery table and he easily succumbs to having the intravenous catheter placed. We all sing our typical song as the drugs are given slowly. We do this for every surgery. Anyone who has ever worked in my hospital knows this protocol. This superstition started 40 years ago and will remain as long as I am the director.

"Lullaby and good night, go to sleepy bye, dear Dexterrrr, it's okaaay, it's alright, go to sleeeepy bye dear Dexterrr. It's okaaay, it's alright, go to sleeeepy bye, dear Dexter, it's okay, it's alright, go to sleepy bye dear Dex."

He slips into a relaxed state and as his heart rate and respiration are being assessed, the endotracheal tube is placed and inhalant anesthesia is started.

137

Steve is too nervous to assist, so I send him off to run errands and walk dogs for two hours. Lindsey is smiling in the background at his antics. A very good client and friend, Dr. Ted Polgar, a human periodontist, is unrelenting in his approach to helping people with periodontal disease and preventing heart related problems that can be connected with it. I am truly honoring his dogma (no pun intended) on this day with Dex and proceed to thoroughly evaluate his mouth and throat. The teeth are heavily stained and covered with stone like calcified plaque. The mandibular incisors are worn to the gum line and loose. Premolars on both sides of his lower jaw have root exposure but are firmly embedded in the periosteal bone. After removing the "rotten" incisors, I begin a thorough cleaning, which takes approximately one and a half hours. His teeth are polished and I move on to examine his right rear foot, which he has been subtly dragging since we adopted him. For the last few weeks he has been licking the two inside toes, and they are ulcerated and red with dark areas on the nails. I am suspicious of a nailbed infection and submit a culture and sensitivity to determine which medications will work. His foot is x-rayed and there is no bone involvement, so I am thankful. His right ear is cleaned and medicated. Fortunately, his throat appears normal, so I'm thinking that his exaggerated gag reflex on a leash may be due to old trauma, perhaps from being chained outside. Additional bloodwork will be sent out to check his thyroid gland.

It's over now and after clipping his nails (easily accomplished under anesthesia), I tenderly touch all his scars as he slowly awakens. How truly atrocious his existence was I will never know, but he is in a good place now with our pack and ourselves.

He is safe and loved. I wish we could save them all. Brooklyn stays near him as he recovers uneventfully on a soft blanket in his compartment. All is well and Steve looks like he could use a good nap, too – without the anesthesia!

UPSTATE NEW YORK

AUTUMN 2019

The Visit

-Dr. Dru Pollinger

It is Saturday morning, October 12, 2019, and we have only four appointments at the animal hospital. It is a spectacular fall day, sunny, clear, and peak season for foliage. I suggest to Steve that we revisit the locale where Dexter was first sighted.

Our first trip to the area around Bakers Mills was last April on a gray, chilly, rainy day, and we didn't have much time to explore. We stopped at a local shopping plaza in North Creek, hoping someone might be familiar with Dexter's story.

Interestingly, Steve chose to go into a liquor store called Adirondack Spirits, thinking that someone local might be working there. Sure enough, a clerk named Theresa recalled feeding a skinny brown dog hanging around her backyard in early May of 2018.

It was no surprise for us to hear her say that when she put out kibble with ground beef and water, the dog ran away, and only returned after dark to eat it. She was heartbroken, looking at his emaciated body, and was familiar with other sightings of this dog from neighbors, and Facebook.

She never saw him again and wondered about his fate. We told her our story, and we brought him out of the car to meet her in the parking lot. By now, he was accepting of the touch and she began to gently pet him. As her eyes welled up, we realized how many strangers must have attempted to interact with him, some having only kindness in their hearts. There appeared to be a solid middle-class base of caring people in this town, from what she relayed to us in conversation, but in driving the back roads, we could see the hidden poverty. We passed numerous trailers and trash ridden yards. Rampant alcoholism was blatantly obvious by the numerous beer bottles strewn on the front yards of these dilapidated dwellings.

Today, in considering which dogs to take with us, we decided to bring Brooklyn with Dexter. It is apparent to me that Steve had something on his mind by choosing only her. She is the one dog so determined to be at Steve's side, that she will escape any barrier, including a ten-foot highway fence, to be near him. As far as we're concerned, she is also Dexter's greatest protector, although it is apparent that Dexter feels that he is protective of her! Typical guy stuff!

We leave the hospital at noon with Subway sandwiches that we all share in the car on the way! The dogs receive only tidbits of bread – Dexter is not happy!

On this day, our plan is to first drive to the Chatiemac Club. Back in September, we had contacted Dan Hitchcock – a name given to us by Mark Laske. Dan worked for the highway department of Johnsburg, New York, and had spoken to Mark about what he called a "patch beagle" that he encountered lying on the side of the road near and at the Chatiemac Club.

He too, saw a dog in such a distressed state that he went home and had his wife cook bacon, thinking that he could lure him with such

142

a treat. But… he like all the others with good intentions, was unable to capture him. It has taken us almost two hours to reach the infamous dirt road that leads to the Second Pond Trailhead, and ultimately, the Club.

Dealing With Demons

- Dexter

Where are we going? It seems like a long ride, but not as long as when we go to Maine and have a fun time. I hope Pop opens the window a bit, so I can get a scent of where we are heading. Pop's energy is different today. He is always so strong, but I sense he is a bit nervous.

As if reading my mind, he opens the window. I know where we are! Why are they bringing me back to this place, where I had so much fear? Have I done something wrong? Mom and Pop would never dump Brooklyn in the woods, or any of my new brothers and sisters, but this is definitely the place where I came from.

My body quivers as I anticipate danger. We turn onto a bumpy dirt road. Mom is giving directions aloud and she is watching me intently. The car slows and I remember this spot, where I lay down on the cold ground, in the rain, too tired to lift my head, wanting only to sleep. If Pop lets me out of the car and drives away, I will follow.

I can't be without my family – Brooklyn, Chomper, Malchus and Harvey. Mom says "Second Pond Trailhead" to Pop, as she looks at a sign, above where I was sleeping in the long-ago time. The car begins to move again, slowly.

A tear rolls down my cheek and I relax, as we move further up the road. I love them, and I don't want to be without them anymore. Mom is beginning to cry, as she talks to Pop about how hard it must have been for me. They are both sad, but Brooklyn doesn't understand – she has no knowledge of my past. She simply stares out the windows, at the deep woods passing by.

We finally stop at an old house surrounded by a lake. There is a long porch on one side that is familiar to me. I slept there, in the cold, hoping that someone would bring me food, but no one came.

Today, it is different – it is sunny and warm. I feel safe now, in the car, with my family. An old man, a lot like Pop, comes out of the front door and walks over to our car. I jump into Pop's lap, in the front seat, to feel secure.

My Pop doesn't miss a beat and immediately introduces himself and gets right to the heart of it. He says "Hi, my name is Steve Pollinger, and I'm from the Fair Haven Animal Hospital in Vermont. Do you recognize this brown dog, sitting in my lap?"

Mom begins to tell my story and is asking him a lot of questions. I do not know this man, but he tenderly places his palm on my cheek and says, "Poor baby." My racing heart slows, as I begin to understand what is unfolding before me, in this place. Mom and Pop are trying to authenticate my history and ordeal. As they continue to talk, I learn that this Chatiemac Club and Lodge closes in the cold winter for three months, and that was the time I was there!

The old man tells Pop that he is the caretaker, and he is preparing a spaghetti and meatball dinner for twenty-seven people tonight. That cold afternoon, when I arrived here a year and a half ago, I thought I was never going to move again, without food.

Now, sitting here in Pop's lap, these demons are making me uncomfortable. The old man's touch, just now, was so gentle, but I wouldn't have experienced that then – I was too afraid of people.

I do remember a man driving up while I was sleeping on the porch. No one else was around. He wasn't from this house, and he came with warm food. He had spotted me at the trailhead and tracked me to this spot. He wanted to catch me – so I ran away. "Hey, Mom and Pop – I know you can't hear me, but I want you to understand that this nice man standing in front of you is nothing like some of the angry people that came after me then" I say silently to myself.

Pop is interrogating the man about the poverty in the area and where I may have come from.

I can still sense that he is a bit nervous, but he is regaining his commanding demeanor, in his attempt to get answers. My escape from living under a trailer owned by some maniacal redneck is hazy, and I don't want to remember any of that.

My anxiety is diminishing now, knowing that I will not be left here. The Pop I know is reemerging, as he goes into a tirade about the "Mother...f-----r" who so mistreated me.

Revisiting More of the Past

-Dr. Dru Pollinger

Jim Smith, the caretaker at the Chatiemac Club, who has so graciously answered our many questions, gives us driving directions to the Garnet Hill Lodge. He mentioned that walking the trails would be considerably shorter, but much more difficult to navigate.

We chose to drive and contemplated a walk, later on. The journey to this five-star resort took only fifteen minutes. Along the way, we passed a man walking a donkey, which greatly excited Brooklyn and Dexter! We arrived at this spacious parking lot, and before Steve got out of the car, we talked about hopefully meeting Sebastian Martinez.

Sebastian was the head chef at the resort and a very health-conscious individual, as well!

In our only conversation with him this past spring, he spoke of Dexter, as a little red dog, looking extremely emaciated. Despite the hectic kitchen that he ran, he did in fact find time to prepare a meal for the dog he could see through the window, out back.

Well thought out, he cooked mashed potatoes with gravy, and put blueberries on top, to lure the dog in. Despite his kind gesture, he only found Dexter to be interested in it, as long as he, Sebastian, was a far, far distance from the food. He also spent his own personal time questioning the large staff at the lodge, about where this dog may have come from. Yet again, he told us that no one knew a thing about this

148

stray. One of the maintenance men would have taken him home, but he was totally unprepared for this kind of challenge. Hearing over the phone that Dexter had a forever home, Sebastian was looking forward to meeting the three of us, and finally touching the dog!

As Steve walked into the reception area of this incredibly, lovely lodge, and asked to see the chef, he was quickly apprised of the fact that Sebastian was no longer working there.

He left suddenly two weeks before, to attend to a family emergency in his country of Puerto Rico. He would not be coming back, because he was hired for a more lucrative position at a five-star restaurant in Boston. Returning to the car, Steve gave me the disappointing news and we decided we would contact him via his email address, to let him know that we had missed seeing him but hoped to meet up in the future.

I suggested that we not walk Dexter around the lodge property, as it might evoke some bad memories for him, so we began to drive back down the mountain road, looking forward to a pit stop about a mile away.

We chose to stop at a jewelry maker. She was a lovely middle-aged woman who crafted earrings and bracelets in her home, using garnet from the local mine. Garnet is typically used as a polishing instrument, but when the garnet itself is polished, it is highly desirable, with gold or silver for adornment. I purchased a few items to remember this trip by. As Steve and I left her shop and backtracked toward the highway, the donkey man was gone!

Nearing the main road, we decided to stop and walk the dogs at a local baseball field. We noticed a sandy, flat path leading into the distant mountains – perfect for a nice trek!

Brooklyn and Dex were leashed, and we started out. Thirty feet from the car, both dogs began jumping wildly into the air, licking their paws, and then pushing their faces into the sand.

We had no idea what was happening and grabbed Brooklyn to see why her mouth was bleeding. I felt under her lip and punctured my fingers with something sharp. At first, I thought she had porcupine quills in her mouth, but quickly ascertained that there were small, prickly thorns embedded in her tongue and lips.

I had never seen these before. They were also stuck between her toes and she was angrily biting at them to get them out! Steve was holding Dexter, who had also stepped on them. My husband remained calm and was able to remove the thorns from both dogs, while I was the one yelling about not having any hemostats in the car.

These prickers were on the soles of my sneakers, my shoelaces, and the bottom of my pants – what a mess! I saved them in a Ziploc™ plastic bag to look them up later on the computer.

Realizing we had several hours of nice weather before dark, we look at each other and, as telepathy has it, we agree to walk a trail that had to be typical of Dexter's days in the woods.

Back at the Second Pond Trailhead, we park the car and begin our hike. We were tempted to let Brooklyn run off lead, but not

Dexter, for he might get confused recalling the sights and smells of his previous life

When they are individually leashed with twenty-foot extensions, the two of us feel that we are about to immerse ourselves in Dexter's history. Off we go.

I look over at Steve who begins to sob uncontrollably and gently pet Dex at the same time. He has taken to Dexter, so much so, that I am beginning to worry about him. God forbid he ever runs into the fellow who originally owned him....

Reliving the Nightmare

-Dexter

"Follow me, Brooklyn," I say to my canine mentor. "I will show you the places I've been and the agony I faced constantly looking for food. There was danger around every turn and I was scared and alone."

Mom and Pop and Brooklyn and I follow the trail into the woods for a quarter mile. And then I stop dead in my tracks and sniff the ground around me.

My silent conversation with Brooklyn continues, telling her what I experienced here long ago. I know she is listening...and that she cares.

"Brooklyn...an animal smell came from behind that tree and my nose lead me to a wounded squirrel. My hunger overtook my senses and I approached without caution, confronting an angry pair of raccoons intent on eating it. Their hisses and strange noises didn't deter me from attempting to devour this long-awaited meal. They bit fiercely and scratched at my face and ears – just look at my scars, Brooklyn. I fought back hard, despite the pain. A tangled mass of teeth and fur – we competed for the prize. If I had not won, my body could not have carried me any further. The food warmed my aching stomach and I moved on, taking shelter in the brambles, where no one could find me. Sleep came quickly."

A Harrowing Encounter

-Dr. Dru Pollinger, Dexter & Brooklyn

We spend a few minutes observing the two dogs interacting on the edge of the path, and then proceed to meander further for another half hour. Once again, Dexter stops, and simultaneously, Brooklyn begins to sniff the air. A huge porcupine ambles out of the woods. The dogs are focused on the critter and are silently communicating with one another.

-Dexter

Brooklyn, that animal is not to be reckoned with. I saw that deadly tail once before. That porcupine whacked a curious fawn with it and the baby deer leaped across the trail into the woods, crying for its mom to take the needles away!

-Dr. Dru Pollinger

We all remain calm. Brooklyn, who has had previous encounters with quills, looks toward Dexter.

-Dexter & Brooklyn

My silent conversation with Brooklyn continued with her telling me that one evening, when Pop's friend was up at the house, she was allowed to walk down our road with him, off leash. She saw a bigger porcupine than this one and thought Dad would want her to take care of the situation.

"As I went for the throat, there were screams coming from this animal," said Brooklyn. "Pop could hear the commotion and came running out the front door. He called me to come immediately. I listened to him and thought he wanted me to bring the porcupine to his feet, which I did, carrying him up the driveway, in my mouth. Pop was not mad at me, but we had to go back to the animal hospital so Mom could pull the quills out of my bleeding face. It took three hours! He saved the dead porcupine to show me, as a reminder to never do it again. I remember that pain and I appreciate your story."

-Dr. Dru Pollinger

The dogs watch quietly while the porcupine continues his journey and moves out of sight, not interested in us. We move along the path for another half mile and recognize that we are now about an hour away from the car. The sun hangs low in the sky and it is important to get back to our other dogs at the animal hospital. Turning around, we head back the way we came, picking up our pace.

Suddenly, the sound of a four-wheeler can be heard coming toward us, and a man's voice calls out from the woods. "Move, I want to get through," he says gruffly. As he comes into view, I notice his torn camouflage jacket and red neck bandana.

In an instant, he stops in front of us. The dogs are barking loudly, sensing some threat. They lunge forward on their leashes toward him and we pull them back to our side.

"Don't let that fucking beagle off leash to chase rabbits – I'm hunting them!" Looking at Steve directly, he pulls out a beer, pops the cap and takes a gulp. He says in a slurred voice, "Did you hear me? I'm talkin' to you!"

Steve hands off Brooklyn's leash to me and I am now holding both animated dogs. I'm getting a queasy feeling in the pit of my stomach. It has been a beautiful day and we have encountered many interesting people, and now this. I am sensing danger, and I tense up.

Steve never backs down and has never lost a fight in which he was a willing participant. His eyes dart from Dexter, to Brooklyn, to me, and I can feel the rage coming over him. We've had Brooklyn for nine years and this is the first time I've seen her growling and showing teeth. Dexter, in my other hand, now begins to cower and he crouches down on the ground near my feet, watching Brooklyn. I know I cannot hold Brooklyn much longer, as she is morphing into the classic angry Pitbull that people fear.

Steve abruptly commands her to stop and she does so immediately. This is all happening within a split second; however, a nightmare scenario is unfolding before my eyes and seems to last forever. A deafening silence ensues.

Steve relaxes his posture and I recognize that he is preparing to do battle. I am unsure what will happen next, as the man takes another gulp of his beer and spits. Once again, Steve looks at the three of us motionless by his side, but this time, his gaze is upon me first, then Brooklyn, and lastly Dexter, where it lingers.

He turns to this unkempt figure, a rifle visible behind his seat in the four-wheeler, and begins to speak.

"We didn't realize that hunting was permitted in this area. We're taking the dogs and going back to our car."

I breathe a sigh of relief and we quickly work our way along the trail as dusk approaches. The sound of the four-wheeler engine revs up and fades in the distance.

No words are spoken between us for a long while. I knew he backed down to avoid any possibility of the three of us being hurt. He is truly the good man that I married.

The Importance of Conversation

-Dr. Dru Pollinger

Dexter has been with us for more than a year and many of our clients have become enamored with his story. They frequently ask to see him and pet him in the waiting room. Their conversations with Steve often include questions about how our family ended up in Vermont.

He tells them the story of my first practice experience, where I worked in a hospital that employed seven veterinarians. My mentor, the practice owner, was running a business first, as he saw it. At the end of my first year there, he congratulated me on the fact that I had generated the most revenue.

He applauded my ability to interact with the clients, and I was delighted to hear that. This accolade came with a caveat. His critique was that I was spending too much time with each client visit, and by shortening each appointment, more income would be generated for the business. I was disconcerted.

The reason I took my time was because an animal's history is seventy percent of the diagnosis and my interaction with owners was beneficial in formulating a plan for their pet's wellness. When I recounted my year end conversation with my boss to Steve, his feeling was that we should open our own hospital, where we could set the rules, and my time constraints would be lifted.

158

A year later, we did just that. Steve made some financial investments that helped ease any monetary issues that came before us.

I was then able to build a client base in a way that I saw fit, with my husband overseeing the day-to-day operation of the clinic. Steve became an integral part of the hospital patient experience.

So I was not surprised one afternoon, when Steve was told a heart wrenching story by a landsman, involving a couple not known to us. This gentleman thought that there were profound similarities in our lifestyles and felt compelled to talk to Steve about their narrative.

Perhaps Steve needed to hear this, because having worked so hard with Dexter and being consumed with his abusive past, he had distanced himself from the animal tragedies that others have faced.

The names of this couple have been changed to preserve their anonymity. Mark Glassberg and his wife had been married for many years. He had successfully run a business which allowed him to retire five years ago.

This couple had a home in the country with significant acreage and lovingly cared for their pack of four dogs. Like Steve, he was self-taught in the art of training and all were impressed by his dogs' behavior.

An unfortunate car accident limited his ability to take the long walks with his pack of which he was so proud. To compensate, he and his wife decided to build an inground lap pool for the dogs' exercise and enjoyment. As the story went on, the footprint for the pool had been dug out with heavy equipment over a period of several days.

On this particular afternoon, possibly intrigued by the new terrain, his alpha dog decided to explore the bottom of the hole with two other pack members. The three dogs were able to jump down easily and to navigate the pit bottom, but it was impossible to climb their way out due to the depth and pitch of the sides. This unfolded moments prior to the cement truck backing up to pour the base for the pool. The sounds of the dogs barking were muffled by the noise of the cement truck mixer.

The owners were inside the house, unaware of the dogs' predicament. When Mark called them to come in, he was baffled when they did not appear at the door. After four hours of searching the property, no dogs returned, and as he considered the possibility of what had transpired, he began to vomit. Night lights were brought in and the cement base of the pool was jack hammered. The unthinkable had happened.

He sat with his older remaining dog in utter disbelief, looking over the edge of the pool he had so lovingly designed. Steve was asked by the client telling the story to meet with and console this couple. He was so distraught by the nature of this tragedy that he did not mention Dexter's name to me for five days.

We talked about this horrific situation later that evening. We both agreed that as careful as we try to be with our pack of five dogs, things can happen in an instant. It reinforced our need to be even more vigilant.

Dogs Need Answers (DNA)

-Dr. Dru Pollinger

In mid-fall of 2019, one of our dear clients, Malcolm Swogger, who had recently adopted a rescue from down south, came into the animal hospital with a thick folder from the dog DNA company, EMBARK. He was ecstatic to find out the genetic information on his new dog and wanted us to put a copy in "Katie's" medical file. He couldn't stop talking about how user friendly and exciting the web site was!

That night at dinner, we wondered why it took us so long to investigate Dexter's lineage. From the get-go, there were many differing opinions as to the type of dog he was. Most people, including ourselves, felt that he fit the description of a beagle/lab cross.

Although he had that appearance, beagles were bred to be hunting dogs, often with their nose to the ground, easily distracted by smells and noises. Dexter does not exhibit this behavior. He also does not chase smaller animals and gets along well with our two cats.

We ordered the EMBARK kit the next morning, after researching numerous dog DNA companies and decided that EMBARK was the most respected. Six days later we were swabbing Dexter's mouth with the cotton applicator provided by them!

We spent the next several weeks anxiously awaiting the results. We even polled our clients as to their thoughts. The company website kept us updated with the progress of the sample and we enjoyed the interaction. Initially we were told it could take six weeks, but the big surprise came earlier with an announcement via email. Steve was aware that the results were in but would not open them until we were both together. The company's presentation with a breed reveal video was so exciting that we now suggest them to everyone!

AND THE WINNER IS!!!:

39.7% Treeing Walker Coonhound

24.4% Rottweiler

12.9% Cocker Spaniel

8.7% Bluetick Coonhound

14.3% Supermutt (Collie, Dalmatian)

Our jaws dropped for different reasons! Steve nearly fell over in his chair with the Rottweiler description (not his favorite breed), and he was considering renaming Dexter to Homer, as the Treeing Walker Coonhound appears to be more recognized as a southern dog. He was just being silly. I was thrilled with the 12.9% Cocker Spaniel, as I love Dexter's sweet round eyes and soft face and could visualize that breed resemblance. No Beagle and no Labrador!

The company also includes a list of potential genetic diseases associated with the breeds, which can be helpful to owners. Dexter had a clean slate. They also provide updates every few weeks of dogs that may resemble Dexter's DNA. As much as we were interested in Dex's genetic makeup, now THEIR staff is interested in reading Dexter's book! We had a happy ending to a new relationship.

Outside the Box

-Steve Pollinger

Traditional training therapy doesn't work for every dog. If a mentally challenged canine is supported by a strong social network—good solid humans and well socialized pack members—they might move through their own healing process naturally, by using the people and other dogs around them as needed.

Interrupting that natural progression by forcing a dog to submit to a regimented training session with a stranger can be counterproductive. Their traumatic memories may be activated longer than the dog can handle. They need to have choice in their interaction.

Not to brag, this was exactly my theory on the day I met Dexter. So, as Frank Sinatra sang to me in my imagination, "I did it my way!" Immediately upon seeing the dog, I realized that he had had no social network, physically or emotionally, to fall back on.

Had Dexter had an owner, master, or family with any sense of goodness or decency, his terror of people would not have been off the charts. I also surmised in the first two days that he may not have had any encounters with aggressive dogs, for he was able early on to relate to and socialize well with our pack.

I have experienced finding lost dogs, who were obviously traumatized as Dexter was, but not to the degree that he exhibited. A case mildly similar to Dexter's happened several years ago, where a

164

dog, lost in the woods and frantic, ran in front of us across a heavily traveled two lane country road.

It was late fall, and Dru and I were returning from a shopping trip to the Tommy Hilfiger outlet store in Lake George. Brooklyn was in the back seat with her service dog jacket; the store employees knew her well from past visits and loved to see her come in with us. Out of nowhere, a large bloodhound ran across the road in front of the car and disappeared into the trees. We immediately pulled over onto the dirt shoulder. There were other cars that had obviously stopped before us.

The dog darted out again, crossing in the opposite direction. Remember my "BURGEONING STEVE" story, at the beginning of the book? Well here we go again! The police soon arrived. We could see that the hound was retreating into the woods when Good Samaritans approached on foot to grab him. The policeman blocked off the road with his vehicle but he was baffled by how to catch the fearful canine. We spoke with him briefly and he was willing to stay the course and allow us to initiate a plan. We had leashes in the car (we always do) and noticing that the bloodhound was an intact male, we decided to use Brooklyn as bait.

Now, with an audience of people in cars on both sides of the road, Brooklyn was trotted out to work her magic – which she was more than willing to do! We knew the male would approach her from behind, and we readied our slip-lead for the encounter. Typical guy dog – BA DA BING – he was leashed at our side and handed off to the policeman.

Remember, the police always take a lost dog! As we walked back to the car, Steve was pointing to Brooklyn, with a smile on his face, and onlookers began applauding her! She wagged her tail and danced around – obviously enjoying the accolades. The rescue occurred over a forty-minute time period, which required our patience as well as the patience of all the vehicles that were forced to stop. Upstate New Yorkers are a bit different on the road than those traveling East River Drive in NYC! Funny though how things come full circle.

Looking Back

-Dr. Dru Pollinger

As we examined our efforts over the last two years to normalize Dexter's dog life, we've reached our own conclusions about methods to deal with PTS.

We now know that major turnarounds are achievable. Yes, one can look at a finite number of ways to teach a young puppy to come, easily. However, defeating demons, no matter what the cause, requires highly individualized rehabilitation. Every human being and dog have a unique personality based on their life experience.

The ability to overcome their mental handicaps takes just the right mentor for their recovery. What we needed to do in Dexter's case, rather immediately, was to ascertain as best we could what his major fears were.

Between us, we surmised the following about him:

He had never been socialized—he had no knowledge of verbal commands.

He had never been inside a home.

He had never been on a leash.

He had no concept of comfort.

A hand approaching his face terrorized him.

He did not exhibit play behavior.

He was bodily scarred from either other animals or human torture or both.

He had underlying medical problems which needed to be addressed.

He did not bark (no one would believe this today)!

On the upside, we could acknowledge the following:

He never showed any aggressive tendencies.

He had a wonderful interest in food – probably from being deprived or starved.

His ability to watch and observe quickly became apparent.

He had obviously spent time with other dogs.

Our initial plan was to allow him to move around the hospital space freely day and night. The irony is that we had ten dog kennels available to house him when we weren't directly interacting with him, but we deliberately chose not to go that route.

While living at the hospital he had free access to the outdoors. We gave him CHOICE, hoping at some point that he would want to be with us. Our patience was unending, our time with him was unlimited and our ultimate goal was to provide a secure, nurturing, and stimulating environment. When we were in the hospital working, we were continually attempting to engage him with our voice, our eyes, and with food treats.

I Am Dexter

We never scolded or raised our voice to him – never. It took hundreds of hours for him to accept being leashed, but it was our time and who was counting? We weren't concerned with other people's opinions because our formula for success was working. His progress was slow but evident.

The first major breakthrough was Dexter allowing me to touch his muzzle while I held his food bowl. How many normal dogs allow that? This was followed by Dexter choosing to be with Steve on the sofa in the animal hospital and allowing him to gently touch his neck.

He showed us through his body language and startle response that there had never been any good touch in his life – only physical abuse. Another major accomplishment occurred when he was finally able to be properly leash walked. As awkward as it appeared initially, it meant to us that eventually he would learn how fulfilling that could be. Exercise first! Steve was unwavering in his confidence to make this happen – he was not bound by time constraints, because he is his own boss and makes his own decisions, as long as I am part of the equation!

At the present time, as he continues to work with Dex on a daily basis, he is hoping to enter an obedience trial with him a year from now, as long as Dexter enjoys the training. Can you believe that? We gave up our social life for years, but we received a remarkable dog in return. Another big step for Dex was his ability to integrate himself into our pack after we observed his desire for canine companionship. Despite one misstep with Malchus in the beginning, we made our pack mentality work. Brooklyn always comes through for us! Lastly, Dexter was able to communicate with us through his bark and his wonderful gaze.

Steve respected Cesar Millan's philosophy that "his way (Cesar's) was not the only way," as long as your goal is accomplished. We both paid homage to Cesar's tenant of exercise, discipline, and affection last.

The fact that we raised five children and found work/family balance despite our schedules helped us with our dog family. Many of the same rules applied.

We ate together every night. We took Sundays for family time and addressed our children's diverse needs together, as they arose – in the same way we raised our dogs. If the kids were crazy on a long car ride, we would find a playground for an hour of fun and exercise The discipline was then sitting calmly in the back seat. We had a wonderful time eating together in the car after stopping for snacks and enjoying the ride on a full stomach! I'm sure we broke the rules of the "experts," both human and canine, but our way worked. For those individuals, whose world revolves around animals, their wide-eyed compliments to us, with respect to our pack, says it all.

WHITEHALL, NY WINTER 2020

REFLECTIONS OF THE PAST

Why Dexter? Why Dru?

-Dr. Dru Pollinger

On February 1, 2011, our youngest son died from a drug overdose. He was 19 years young—smart, a great athlete, handsome, and loving. Tommy had never wanted to disappoint his mom and dad. Part of me died that day too. Over a long period of time and with the help of my family, my community, my job, and my animals, I have forgiven myself for not being able to save my boy.

On August 6, 2018, Steve brought Dexter into the animal hospital and within hours of observing this pathetic creature, I knew I could not let him down. I was one hundred percent committed to rehabilitating him with Steve. On a conscious level, I began using the knowledge of my own healing process to help Dex live his life.

On that first evening I made Dexter's meal with attentiveness and love. Years before our neighbors and friends did that for us as we attempted to heal. I mixed the kibble and cooked chicken livers with my hands slowly, while he watched from a distance staring blankly. I took my time, thinking of what he must have been through. I placed it before him, hoping he would devour it and he did. He was a survivor with a will to live.

Well-wishers performed countless considerate deeds after Tommy died, that we were unaware of for a long time. The farmer down the road had asked the local radio station to play church music in Tommy's name several Sundays in a row. Cards came in the mail for many weeks with heartfelt thoughts that I took great solace from. Now, our dogs were becoming Dexter's community of friends. Without them I don't believe we could have helped him so effectively. I hoped that Brooklyn, Chomper, Harvey and Malchus would teach Dex how to be a part of a team and they did so invisibly. He learned from them. We realized as time passed that he had picked up on their habits from simply observing their behavior.

My clients, attempting to console me years ago, talked to me about their own personal tragedies and recounted stories about their connection to my son. His friends, as they became responsible adults, brought their own pets in for veterinary care.

After Dexter's arrival, these same people wanted to help him heal as well. He needed to be socialized and by living in the hospital he was introduced to new people every day. They enjoyed meeting him, watching his evolution over time, and eventually being able to pet him. People in nearby stores wanted Steve to bring him in so they could see his progress. Dexter became a local fixture, walking the sidewalks with Steve – people honking at him from their cars as they drove by!

Looking back over time, I realize above all, how much the hugs of heartfelt sympathy meant to me. It was a personal connection for a moment that let me know people cared. Dexter needed this "good touch" feeling as well. This became the hardest task of all to accomplish. It took months for him to allow us to be to be less than 10 feet away before he would attempt to retreat to another room. I could be close to him when he was eating, but that was it.

I would kneel and softly talk to him, I would entice him with treats, I would simply sit quietly and not move. Gradually, the distance between us shortened, but reaching for him was forbidden! It wasn't until Steve began taking naps on the sofa in the hospital that Dex chose to lie down on the floor close to his arm. I knew then that he was choosing to be near us.

When we finally brought him home and he began sleeping on the sofa first, and then the bed, he allowed us to slowly pet him. Perhaps from watching us pet the other dogs or because he was understanding "good touch" for the first time – we could see him in a relaxed state. FINALLY!!

For years, being at the animal hospital during the day and watching TV crime shows at night helped to muffle the noise in my head. If I were not actively engaged in work or focused on someone else's predicament, memories of my son's life would surface. I realized from day one, that Dexter needed distraction too, and ultimately to have a job. I noticed that he began to watch me continuously during the day. He would sit at a distance, perhaps in a doorway, and stare. He could sit like this for an hour or more, it was a TV show for him.

The number of people and animals coming into his space was entertainment that he could choose on his own. He picked the TV station. He could leave and go into the backyard if he decided to, or he could watch all the activity in the exam rooms. I also left the radio on for him all night in the animal hospital, hoping the noise would muffle his anxiety.

I Am Dexter

The job came last. It was only after he found his voice and could communicate with us on a verbal level, that his "profession" became evident. He was the great protector! Despite having four other vigilant dogs, Dexter was the ultimate pack leader when it came to alerting us of danger – or what he perceived as danger. Danger was anything new – new dogs, new people, new noises, new places. This created self-esteem.

So really, I never had a second thought about helping this dog. Just as I learned to live my life again, Dexter did too. He will forever be "a work in progress," but then so will I. We helped each other on our healing journey.

Why Dexter? Why Steve?

-Steve Pollinger

In the beginning, I wanted to work my magic as a trainer with a dog that had serious behavioral problems. When Florence called that day, I thought it was simply an interesting case that would make me look kind of special! Little did I realize, in our first encounter, how much Dexter reminded me of my younger self. Then and there, I had the deepest desire to make him whole again and in turn this endeavor became my catharsis.

It's 2 o'clock on a Saturday afternoon – the coldest day yet of this new year. My plan was to finish my portion of the book today. My feelings are so deep-rooted that it has taken me a glass of wine early in the day (which I never do) and a phone call to one of my most cherished friends – George Cohen (93 years old) to write down my "seventh veil" thoughts.

There was a period of my life when I was extremely shy and self-doubting. George was one of the people who enabled me to gain the confidence that I have today. He was one of several men that mentored me in my youth at a very vulnerable time. Had I not met any of them, I would most certainly be dead, or in prison. So, what I saw in Dexter – the fear, the lack of trust, the abuse that he must have suffered, triggered a visceral response in me to give him my all. Let me explain further.

176

I Am Dexter

At the age of twelve, I was trying to overcome the mental trauma of a frightening encounter with a sexual predator. It's too difficult to be any more graphic. Simultaneously, as a young Jewish boy in Brooklyn walking a mile to Hebrew school, Torah in hand, I was physically assaulted daily by a sidewalk gang of thugs.

After numerous visits to the police station where I was repeatedly questioned about the altercations, I was introduced to a lieutenant who coached boxing in his spare time. Feeling sorry for my circumstance, he took me under his wing.

After a year of training in the gym, without missing a single night, I was in the ring participating in a boxing match with one of the gang members. A first-round knockout gave me the confidence to consider a boxing career. The intense physical activity created a mindset that made me mentally strong and physically capable.

Unfortunately, by the time I was sixteen, all those early horrors resurfaced in my mind. I found myself beating up anyone who looked at me the wrong way, even on a subway platform. Recognizing that I had become too aggressive, which I knew was wrong, I found a psychiatrist who worked with young people and he helped to turn me around.

He was gentle and compassionate. I remember Boris saying to me in our first session, "I know you can beat me up, so what?" He became my second mentor. We kept in touch long after our sessions ended, until his untimely death at a young age.

Recognizing that Dexter had been mentally and physically abused created an immediate bond. A fierce instinct arose in me to protect him forever. Dexter needed the physical activity of long daily disciplined walks to calm his mentation and allow his fears to dissipate, just like me.

Dexter never exhibited aggression. In contrast, the continued fear in his eyes was killing me. Throughout the book, this is why I say, "God help the people that originally owned him!"

He too, needed someone with a gentle presence and calm assertive energy to turn him around. In my sage, advanced years, I knew I could accomplish that! It was important in Dexter's evolution for him to finally learn how to have fun, after being maligned for so long in his past life.

In my early twenties I had become too serious after facing my own demons and was encouraged by George, who was my first boss, to lighten up and have fun with the people I encountered on a daily basis. He taught me business manners and social etiquette as well, which has stayed with me forever. Could I now transfer these lessons to Dexter? Helping him to lose his fear of people and places would be the precursor of his being able to enjoy our interactions together.

I used my very personal life experiences to help Dexter become the dog he was meant to be – a silly, stubborn, vocal, highly intelligent little brown dog. In the process, I became more whole. Has Dexter been normalized? Pretty much so. Is he having a good time? YOU BETCHA!

FAIR HAVEN, VERMONT

SOMETIME IN THE FUTURE

Imagining the Underdog Becoming a Champion

-Steve & Dr. Dru Pollinger and Dexter

-Steve

"I can't believe we took third, Dexter – I can't believe we took third! I feel like choking that judge! This was the best performance I ever could have expected of you. Your eyes were so focused on me and you followed those commands better than I would have, if I were you."

-Dexter

Why are your crying, Pop? It doesn't really matter!

I had a grand time with you – how did you like that last sit/stay for 10 minutes?

-Steve

"It matters a lot to me. The politics of these contests are so outrageous. Did you have lunch with the judge? Do you come in with a reputation? Do you agree with him/her politically? Are you fostering the cause for a particularly fashionable breed? Did I wear the wrong outfit? I know both our gaits are a bit off, as they always are because of our physical handicaps, but that wasn't what this contest was about.

It really was about you and I connecting, and that overrated judge had made the decision before we even walked into the ring. We got robbed! Hey Dex – do you remember when you were barking at me when we were doing the lure coursing in the front yard 3 years ago? You wouldn't stop barking because you understood what you needed to do to win the game. I learned from you! Dru – I'm going to go over to that judge and let her know how I feel!"

-Dexter to Dru: …. barking:

Calm Pop down – let him know it's okay!

-Steve

"You know, they chose that golden retriever and I saw him look away from his master – and the black lab that came in second, was jogging when he was supposed to walk! How could I get cheated like this?"

-Dru To Steve

"For almost 50 years I've been telling you to calm down! Did you not have a good time?"

-Steve

"All the women came over to me and thought Dex was the cutest and most obedient. If they thought he won, where was that judge's head? Ah, what the hell – I had a great time!"

We go back to the house after an emotional day with Dexter and relax on the couch. For some unknown reason, I began thinking about the older couples that came to the animal hospital over the years, facing necessary euthanasia for their beloved pets; and all the time they spent together, navigating the ups and downs of life.

As Dru and I tried to console them and talked of their future, perhaps with another dog, I thought of Dexter's life and talked about him. Always, the conversation terminated with their concern about falling in love with another dog and facing the fact that they may die first, leaving a beloved pet in a precarious situation – with an unknown outcome

I find myself at my age understanding that thought process. Ten years ago, I was so upbeat in trying to soften their pain by encouraging them to form a new bond. Now, I have worries about the future too!

My wife always says that our brain wiring changes every 10 years, and our thoughts about life undergo a metamorphosis. Would I have taken Dexter in now, years later – even knowing the wonderful success

182

I would have, or would I worry as our clients did about who would pass first? I'm beginning to feel that I was naïve in not understanding their very deep emotions.

Dru and I have had these thoughts from time to time as our pack ages with us. I don't want to sound too maudlin, so I now make a conscious choice on this day of a loss, win (in my mind) to live for the now and reflect on my wonderful journey with Dex.

A Wide-Eyed Look Into the Future

-Dexter

We're free now – no leashes, on a beautiful trail beyond the sheep pasture on our own land! We are all together, always. We don't go to the animal hospital anymore. We can sleep in with Mom and Pop. They are retired, whatever that means.

Sometimes, Chomper has been staying alone at the house because it is too hard for him to walk the path. It's hard for Pop now, too. I've seen him fall a couple times on the soft ground. I try to help him when he's down but he always says, "I'll get myself up," and he counts to three and pushes himself up. He does that getting up from the sofa, too!

He's fixing the four-wheeler and building a cart to tow behind, so Chomper doesn't keep missing all the fun. Pop will have an easier time too – sitting in the driver's seat! Mom walks along next to us with a big stick. She gets us all mixed up when she calls out our names – I wonder if she has that canine cognitive dysfunction syndrome? I know this stuff because I listened when she talked to people about their dogs at the animal hospital.

And then I sit with my pack, whom I have come to love so much and we have one of our silent but serious conversations:

"Dex, you know this four-wheeler business reminds me of that time we went to see where you came from," says Brooklyn.

"What do you mean where did I come from?" I ask. "I came from Mom and Pop, just like you. I have papers now – my DNA is legit."

"You fool, Dex, don't you remember North River and the Adirondacks? Brooklyn told me all about it." Malchus says.

I think long and hard before I respond. "I remember the animal hospital and the back yard, the donuts, my sofa, Lindsey, the noisy moving scale, the office, the Dog Day Center, my walks, my car rides, my backrubs, the doors, the windows. I remember Pop teaching me how to be a dog without agita and to be trustworthy and loyal. I remember training for an obedience trial that Pop is going to enter us in – something you never did. I also remember Mom singing and Dad slipping me treats, the trips to Maine, my birthdays, Thanksgiving turkey, my cats, my peanut butter, the TV, my leash, my sheep. And then there's Subway, the bank, the drug store, the supermarket, Destiny at the Liberty. So, my memory is better than yours, Malchus!"

I continue telling them, "people reach out to pet me everywhere I go now and I like it. They say how cute I am. I remember my pack, my big bed with Mom and Pop, my breakfast nibbles, my lunch bites, Mom cooking my dinner on the stove and my pee tree. I know how to walk nicely and play with a stick, and I can dance! I watch now like always, but I AM NOT AFRAID.

By the way, Malchus – I don't dig big holes like you, and I don't hoink Brooklyn. I don't shred sticks like Brooklyn and I don't jump on Mom's lap all the time like Harvey, and when I take my treats, I don't bite somebody's hand off like Chomper. And Chomper, just so you know – you can't HEAR anymore!"

I can feel it in my heart.... Mom and Pop think I am special, and I know they like me the best – look at all the books with my picture on the cover and look at my framed picture on the wall in the house! Do you know why? Because...

I AM DEXTER!

Yes, I do remember things... but the Adirondacks?

Only one rainy day in a ditch on the side of the road,

waiting for a rainbow with a pot of gold at the end...

and I found it.

The End

EPILOGUE

As we write this book in 2021, Dexter has now been living with us for three years. His transformation from petrified and abused animal into happy and loving pet...and truly a member of our pack family, has been transformational for us as well. We could never have imagined the impact Dexter would have on our lives. We can't envision life without him...he has done so much to heal our souls too. He has found his forever home and his journey to us is truly a miracle.

We hope this story will inspire others to consider helping and rescuing dogs and cats who are desperately in need of loving kindness. You just may discover ...as did we... you will be rescued in return.

-Steve and Dru

About the Authors

Steve Pollinger has worked with dogs and studied animal behavior for over forty years. His niche is successfully rehabilitating beaten-down dogs. As co-owner of the Fair Haven Animal Hospital in Vermont; his challenging work continues daily as he interacts with clients and their pets. As a parallel skill, during the course of his life, he has mentored young teenagers that have been bullied; by working with them in and out of the boxing ring. This kind of teaching includes empowering discussions that promote self-esteem. Steve studied acting in his youth at the New School for Social Research in Manhattan, New York and that talent has enabled him to communicate with people from many walks of life. Literary writing was also part of the curriculum and thankfully so, as writing this book has been both purposeful and meaningful! Steve then continued his education with an emphasis on business management; and is a graduate of Kingsboro College in Brooklyn, New York.

Having grown up on the streets of Brooklyn, he is comfortable in both urban and rural settings This book is the culmination of his lifelong dream of conveying positive attitude in working with both people and their canine companions. It is the first in a series of four that will be written over the next few years. He currently resides with his wife, veterinarian Dr. Dru Pollinger and many assorted critters in Whitehall, New York and can be reached at the Fair Haven Animal Hospital, Fair Haven, VT..

Dr. Dru Pollinger, VMD has been a solo veterinary practitioner in rural Fair Haven, Vermont for nearly forty years, where she and her husband Steve co-own the Fair Haven Animal Hospital. She received a B.A. degree in Biology from Bryn Mawr College, an M.S. degree in Microbiology from the University of Tennessee and a VMD degree from the University of Pennsylvania School of Veterinary Medicine. She also worked in the Bovine Leukemia Research Laboratory at New Bolton Center in Kennett Square, Pennsylvania. Dru has been a hard-working lifelong quiet achiever -a lover of mountain views and mother nature. She enjoys a good cup of coffee in the morning and PB&J on a toasted English Muffin. Dru and Steve …together always, raised five children, and are currently overseeing their five dogs, three cats and ten sheep on fifty pristine acres on a mountaintop in Whitehall, New York where they cherish their privacy. Needless to say, she is an over-the-top animal lover, loyal and dedicated to her family, clients, and their pets. As a woman with a glass-half-full mentality, the positivity she radiates enables her to always have hope for the future.

Helayne Rosenblum achieved a B.A.in Communications & Journalism from the University of Miami in Coral Gables, Her vast professional experience consists of more than two decades of multimedia copywriting.

For more than 17 years she was the Senior Writer/Producer of the nationally syndicated CBS Worldwide Distribution Mr. Food Television News segment, seen by millions of viewers daily on the local network news in over 160 TV markets.. She also wrote content for nineteen of the popular Mr. Food cookbooks.

As owner of HGR Copywriting, she works with clients to help them achieve their content marketing goals. She is a contributing writer to PalmBeachLiveWorkPlay.com and a freelance Senior Writer for StoryTerrace. Helayne is a wife, mother, and grandmother as well as an avid animal lover; over the years having many beloved dogs and cats share her home.

About JEBWizard Publishing

JEBWizard Publishing offers a hybrid approach to publishing. By taking a vested interest in the success of your book, we put our reputation on the line to create and market a quality publication. We offer a customized solution based on your individual project needs.

Our catalog of authors spans the spectrum of fiction, non-fiction, Young Adult, True Crime, Self-help, and Children's books.

Contact us for submission guidelines at

https://www.jebwizardpublishing.com

Info@jebwizardpublishing.com

Or in writing at

JEBWizard Publishing

37 Park Forest Rd.

Cranston, RI 02920